The Semiotics of Culture and Language

Open Linguistics Series

The Open Linguistics Series, to which this two-volume work makes a highly significant contribution, is 'open' in two senses. First, it provides an open forum for works associated with any school of linguistics or with none. Linguistics has recently emerged from a period in which many (but never all) of the most lively minds in the subject seemed to assume that transformational generative grammar—or at least something fairly closely derived from it—would provide the main theoretical framework for linguistics for the forseeable future. In Kuhn's terms, linguistics appeared to some to have reached the 'paradigm' stage. Reality today is very different. More and more scholars are examining approaches to language that were formerly scorned for not accepting as central the particular set of concerns highlighted in the Chomskyan approach—such as Halliday's systemic-functional theory, Lamb's stratificational-relational model and Pike's tagmemics—while others are developing new or partly new theories. The series is open to all approaches, then, including work in the generativist-formalist tradition.

The second sense in which the series is 'open' is that it encourages works that open out 'core' linguistics in various ways: to encompass discourse and the description of natural texts; to explore the relationships between linguistics and its neighbouring disciplines such as semiotics, psychology, sociology, philosophy, artificial intelligence, and cultural and literary studies; and to apply it in fields such as education and language pathology.

This book is 'open' in many of these ways. Some of the papers present the recent thinking of active contributors to systemic-functional and stratificational-relational linguistics, but above all the book constitutes an 'opening out' of linguistics into the broad, inter-disciplinary area of 'semiotics'. It thus makes an important contribution to this increasingly significant discipline.

Open Linguistics Series Editor
Robin P. Fawcett, The Polytechnic of Wales

Modal Expressions in English, Michael R. Perkins
Text and Tagmeme, Kenneth L. Pike and Evelyn G. Pike
The Semiotics of Language and Culture, 2 vols., eds: Robin P. Fawcett, M. A. K. Halliday, Sydney M. Lamb and Adam Makkai
Into the Mother Tongue: A Case Study in Early Language Development, Clare Painter

The Semiotics of Culture and Language

Volume 1
Language as Social Semiotic

Edited by
Robin P. Fawcett
M. A. K. Halliday
Sydney M. Lamb
Adam Makkai

Frances Pinter (Publishers)
London and Wolfeboro N.H.

© Frances Pinter (Publishers) 1984

First published in Great Britain in 1984 by
Frances Pinter (Publishers) Limited
25 Floral Street, London WC2E 9DS

Published in the United States of America in 1984 by
Frances Pinter (Publishers), 27 South Main Street,
Wolfeboro New Hampshire. 03894-2069 USA

British Library Cataloguing in Publication Data
The semiotics of culture and language.—
    (Open linguistics series)
    Vol. 1
    1. Semiotics
    I. Fawcett, Robin P.   II. Series
    401'.9   P99
    ISBN 0-86187-295-9

Library of Congress Cataloging in Publication Data
The semiotics of culture and language.
    (Open linguistics series)
    Bibliography: p.
    Includes index.
    Contents: v. 1. Language as social semiotic—
v. 2. Language and other semiotic systems of culture.
    1. Semiotics.   2. Language and languages.
3. Language and culture.   I. Fawcett, Robin P.
II. Series.
P99 S393   1984   401'.41   83-242230

Typeset by Joshua Associates Limited, Oxford
Printed in Great Britain by SRP Ltd, Exeter

Contents

VOLUME 2 LANGUAGE AND OTHER SEMIOTIC SYSTEMS OF CULTURE

Part II Some semiotic systems other than language

Part III Relating culture and language

List of Figures

List of Tables

Foreword

Semiotics, which I take to be the study of sign systems and their use, is not a subject that has many practitioners who actually *call* themselves 'semioticians' (or 'semiologists' to use the term favoured in the mainland European tradition). On the other hand it could well be argued that the world is full of applied semioticians, in that semiotic issues are inherently involved whenever a language is taught and learned, whenever a linguist studies language in general or a language in particular, whenever a psychologist studies gaze or proxemic behaviour, and whenever a student of art or music or literature is at work. But this is a little different: the student of semiotics is also concerned with the *general* principles of signs and sign systems. And it is perhaps here that we can locate the reason why, so far, semiotics has not captured the imagination of all these unconscious practitioners. It could be, I suggest, that, at each stage of the development of knowledge and for each broad class of phenomena, there is a crucial level of generality that operates. An analogy from the English lexical system would be our preference for the relatively specific terms **car, lorry/truck, bicycle,** etc., instead of **vehicle.** In both cases a key factor is prominence of the sub-categories in the affairs of the social group concerned, and so in its culture. The fact is that there is intense interest in language in society at large—and now increasingly in other specific semiotic systems such as body language—but relatively little, so far, in the general principles of sign systems.

Yet semiotics, it could be argued, is crucial to an understanding of human nature—both social and psychological. For it is the sign systems that we use for interaction with other living beings that determine our potential for thought and social action. Central among these, of course, is language, but other codes that till now have been studied less from a semiotic perspective, such as music and architecture, perhaps have a more important place in our cognitive and social lives than our current cultural prejudices allow. As the Editors' 'Introduction' suggests, one of the main tasks for the second half of the 1980s and of the 1990s may well be to bring the essentially humanistic science of semiotics to bear on the question of the impact on society of the current technology-led revolution in information storage and communication. An awareness of the importance of general semiotic principles could be crucial to the right conduct of this revolution.

The implicit claim of the contributors to this important two-volume work is that linguistics has something very specific to give to semiotics, and that relational network models of language in particular, i.e. systemic and stratificational linguistics, have a fundamental contribution to make. Their claim to this role is a double one. First, they are theories that give a central place in their overall framework to the concept of 'culture' as well as to that of 'language' —as indeed does tagmemics. Second, they make use of a 'network' notation that emphasizes *relationships* rather than *entities*. It is a notation which is certainly equally applicable to modelling language-like semiotic systems, and which may well be equally applicable to modelling culture.

This is an important book, and its two volumes should make a significant impact, both on the burgeoning field of semiotics and on the work of that growing number of linguists who recognize the need for a wider perspective—i.e. the semiotic perspective—in their study of language.

The Polytechnic of Wales   Robin P. Fawcett
February 1984

Introduction

It was three centuries ago that the philosopher John Locke proposed that we should recognize, as one of the three major sub-divisions of science, *semiotic*, 'the business whereof is to consider the nature of signs, the mind makes use of for the understanding of things or conveying the knowledge to others'. The modern term *semiotics*, however, was introduced to the English language only in 1962. It was proposed for this role by the anthropologist Margaret Mead, at an important conference whose scope included the fields of cultural anthropology, education, linguistics, psychiatry, and psychology. The proceedings are reported in *Approaches to Semiotics* (Sebeok, Hayes and Bateson: 1964), and on pages 275-6 we can read how 'semiotics' triumphed over 'communication' as the label for the field that Mead, in words that interestingly complement those of Locke, described as 'patterned communication in all modalities'. Today, however, both labels are in regular use: there are steadily growing numbers of courses and departments of 'communication studies' and 'human communication', while 'semiotics' tends to connote work at a more advanced level.

The conceptual territory proposed for semiotic(s) by Locke, and later claimed for their subject by semioticians such as C. S. Peirce and Charles Morris and others, was truly on the grand scale. And yet, while there has been steady progress in recent years, the promise of Locke's original striking proposal has barely begun to be fulfilled. It may be pertinent to ask why this should be so and, further, to suggest some ways in which we might begin to change this situation. We shall return to this topic in the closing section of this introduction.

The process of change in semiotics has, however, already begun. This can be demonstrated most obviously in terms of the increasing numbers of courses, departments and research centres devoted to this field. But fundamental to this has been the fact that linguistics, anthropology, literary analysis and, perhaps to a lesser extent, social psychology, have begun a historical convergence in the discipline of semiotics. Originally a branch of pragmatist philosophy (*à la* William James and C. S. Peirce), semiotics has undergone considerable changes within this century. The growth of interest in semiotics is evidenced by the setting up, in 1976, of the Semiotic Society of

America, to parallel similar societies in Germany, Poland, Hungary and elsewhere. Earlier, the Association Internationale de Sémiotique had been established, and its journal, *Semiotica* (edited by T. A. Sebeok), has been appearing since 1969. In all these ways, then, we are witnessing the emergence of this vital new and broadly inter-disciplinary field.

However, it is an odd but noteworthy feature of the field that many of its practitioners have been working in it without labelling their efforts as semiotics. There is thus a relatively 'official' field of semiotics, labelled as such and practised by recognized semio-ticians, and a relatively 'unofficial' variety, which includes those with interests in various individual semiotic systems. Among these are an ever-growing number of scholars who are interested in the semiotic exploration of language in relation to other cultural systems that have not been labelled as semiotics. The present work represents in part a statement by practitioners of the latter variety who would now like to claim explicitly that their work, too, qualifies as semio-tics. In so doing they hope to bring some fresh thinking into this fertile field.

For the contributors to this book, an event of particular significance in the development of the semiotic dimension in their work was the Burg Wartenstein Symposium, sponsored by the Wenner-Grenn Foundation for Anthropological Research, held in August 1975. All the contributors were present, and in many cases the papers included here constitute a later and more complex working of ideas first presented there in tentative form. In other cases the papers are completely, or almost completely, different. That symposium was originally planned by Charles Frake, M. A. K. Halliday, Martin Kay, Sydney Lamb and W. C. Watt, and their purpose for it—and so the topic addressed by many of these papers—was summarized in the following background statement, which was sent to all the participants.

It has often been proposed that structural patterns found in language might exist also in other cultural systems, and that analytical tools developed in linguistics might prove illuminating if applied in cultural anthropology; but up to now the nature of linguistic structure has been too poorly understood to enable this proposal to be convincingly demonstrated. Against this background, recent developments in linguistics show promise of providing valuable new techniques in cultural anthropology and new insights into the structure of culture. Thus, perhaps there is now some chance of finally fulfilling the promise of old, and perhaps a firm basis can be established for breaking down the fences that separate linguistics, anthropology, sociology, and psychology.

The basic aim of the symposium is to promote the integration of linguistics and cultural anthropology by exploring (1) the use of methods of formal linguistics (especially relational network analysis) for illuminating our understanding of culture, and (2) the use of cultural and social information for illuminating our understanding of the structure and functions of language.

More particularly, it may be profitable to view the social system as a system of information and, accordingly, to view social interaction as information processing. In keeping with this viewpoint, the relation between language and culture can be considered as a relation between two (possibly intertwined) semiotic systems, the linguistic and the cultural.

The symposium itself was co-organized by M. A. K. Halliday, Sydney Lamb and John Regan, and it was a highly interactive, often very insightful, occasionally frustrating, and always stimulating week. The thanks of all of us go to the Wenner-Grenn Foundation for Anthropological Research, and particularly to Dr Lita Osmundsen, the Foundation's Director of Research, and to the staff at Burg Wartenstein.

It may be of value to indicate some of the ways in which the subsequent work of most of the contributors to that symposium has grown more overtly semiotic. M. A. K. Halliday, for example, published in 1978 his influential *Language as Social Semiotic*. The intertwined topics of language, social context and culture are never far from the centre of his writings, and the courses in the Linguistics Department of the University of Sydney reflect this orientation. So, indeed, do those of his wife Ruqaiya Hasan at Macquarie University. W. C. Watt's interest in semiotics in general and the Roman alphabet in particular has continued in a series of articles entitled 'What is the proper characterisation of the alphabet? I, II and III'. Robin Fawcett has since moved to the Polytechnic of Wales, Cardiff, where he teaches and researches on linguistics in the context of a BA(Hons) Communications Studies degree, in which semiotics plays a unifying role. This is one of half a dozen such courses that have been developed over the last few years in British polytechnics, and the work of Kress, Fiske and others is now leading to the development of similarly academic courses in Australia and the United States. Fawcett's recent *Cognitive Linguistics and Social Interaction* (1980) places language in a cognitive–social (and so cultural) framework that embraces other codes beside language, and in 1982 he gave the Invited Lecture to the Linguistic Association of Canada and the United States, 'Language as a semiological system: a re-interpretation of Saussure'. Michael O'Toole has moved to the Chair of Human Communication at Murdoch University, Perth, Australia, where there are now lively undergraduate courses that give semiotics a central place. Similarly, Sydney Lamb has moved to Rice University, where he has been prominent in the foundation of the new Department of Linguistics and Semiotics—the first in existence—together with the Doctoral Program in Linguistics and Semiotics. It was inaugurated by an important symposium 'Directions in linguistics and semiotics', in March 1983, and contributors included Lamb, Halliday and Preziosi from the Wenner-Grenn Symposium, as well as many other well-known linguists and semioticians, including Conklin, Fillmore, Hockett, Longacre, Ross and Sebeok. The proceedings of that symposium have been published as Copeland (1984). The Rice tradition continued with a second symposium in February 1984, and the participants included, from this book, Fawcett, Halliday, Hasan and Lamb. We could give even more examples, but the above will illustrate how the semiotic dimension is becoming an increasingly strong force, both in the work of the contributors to this volume and in the academic world at large.

This work is arranged in three parts. Volume 1 contains Part I, and volume 2 Parts II and III. The title of Part I is 'Language as social semiotic'—a form of words taken from the title of the well-known book by M. A. K. Halliday mentioned above. Part I offers five perspectives on this topic, and the first, appropriately, is by Halliday himself.

The first part of Halliday's chapter provides an interesting perspective on recent work in linguistics, and so a perspective for the book as a whole. He shows us that linguistics has in recent decades been undergoing a period in which the view of language as code, which he terms the 'logical-philosophical', has for most linguists been divorced from the 'ethnographic-descriptive' view of language as behaviour, but he suggests, significantly, that this should be regarded simply as a temporary phase. Systemic functional linguistics, to the development of which he has been the pre-eminent contributor, can then be seen as a contribution to the search for a 'unified "code-and-behaviour" linguistics'—as indeed can stratificational-relational grammar. So far so good, but where does culture come in? Halliday's answer is that, just as the social context of linguistic *behaviour* is the 'context of situation', so the social context of the linguistic *code* is the 'context of culture' (to use Malinowski's terms). In order to relate the two, Halliday suggests, 'we need to represent the culture as . . . a network of information systems: that is, in semiotic terms.' And he continues: 'the central problem is to interpret language in a way which enables us to relate it to other semiotic processes.' Halliday then illustrates his own approach to this problem: he represents certain aspects of culture relating to the code for dialogue as 'behaviour potential' (using a simple system network) and then in turn relates these to their 'realisation' in networks at the 'semantic' and the 'lexico-grammatical' levels of language. He then comments on some short texts in the light of these proposals, and finally outlines the ontogeny of dialogue as it occurred in the case of a single child (Nigel). These closing sections thus serve as an exemplification of the relationship of culture to language, as Halliday sees it in relation to the dialogue of a child. The chapter also includes a brief addition to his proposals for modality.

John Regan's contribution traces the relationship between teacher and pupil as mirrored in and constructed by the discourse patterns of instruction. A long-time student of the Whorf hypothesis, Regan presents data suggesting that the discourse patterns employed by teachers in various countries—and these exhibit a surprising uniformity—exert a powerful influence on the child's conceptual system, quite apart from the content of the instructional material which is overtly being conveyed.

Yoshihiko Ikegami presents a wealth of evidence exploring the notion that all linguistic expressions of change and state are modelled after those of the most concrete types of change and state, i.e. motion and existence in location. Since this type of meaning ('transitivity' in Halliday's terms, 'cases' in Fillmore's) would, in a Whorfian view of language, be held to be closely bound up with the wider culture of the society using the language in question, the whole paper is, in a sense, concerned with language and culture. He concludes that, although there is clearly a set of common underlying patterns in the linguistic representation of change and state, and that these patterns can very closely be approximated to those for representing motion and location, the claim of universal priority of the localistic notions does not hold.

Jeffrey Ellis proposes a framework for exploring relationships among descriptive linguistics, historical linguistics, and socio-linguistics, with particular reference to the socio-cultural aspects of language contact. He draws extensively upon data of language use in Ghana, including problems of contact between English and native languages, and socio-cultural aspects of the use of English by the British, as opposed to natives who use English as a second language.

Ruqaiya Hasan develops the fascinating concept of semantic distance across languages, using data from English and Urdu, and argues that a culture has a characteristic semiotic style, whose crucial characteristics are reflected in all systems of communication, whether verbal or non-verbal. She concludes that semantic differences between languages cannot be properly studied without consideration of their socio-cultural settings, and moreover that the failure of most testers of the Whorfian hypothesis to properly include such considerations 'effectively bears Whorf out in his assertion that it is a characteristic of the SAE [Standard Average European] cultures to treat the abstract relational notion as a concrete object'. This emphasis on relations as distinct from entities is a concept that is taken up in other papers, most notably Lamb's.

Volume 2 contains both Part II and Part III. If the central object of study in semiotics is semiotic systems, Part II offers three stimulating approaches to fulfilling this task. It is a task that in traditional semiotics has received rather less attention than semioticians coming from a linguistics background might expect. This, then, is one of the ways in which 'semiotically aware' linguists may have something very specific to contribute to the general field of semiotics: the commitment to constructing working grammars that make clear predictions about what will and will not occur when a semiotic system is being employed. Each of the three contributors develops a treatment of a specific cultural system which appears to have structural analogies to language. In two of the cases the analogies are well-known and have received considerable study in the past: writing systems and narrative structures. The third, environmental structure, is less obviously a semiotic system, and is a relative newcomer in this family of related topics.

W. C. Watt frames his study of our system of capital letters within an examination of the case for an area of study to be called 'psycho-semiotics', on the model of 'psycho-linguistics'. He thus brings an explicitly cognitive approach to the study of semiotic systems— an approach taken up again later in the contributions of Lamb and Fawcett. Watt argues for the view that 'for human sign-systems "what people have in their heads" is not a peripheral enquiry: it is the *only* enquiry.' He discusses the nature of evidence and criteria in semiotics, and presents a specific semiotic study of structural patterns in the Roman alphabet. The semiotic system that he is discussing is thus not language itself, strictly speaking, though it is one that relates closely to, and is indeed parasitic on, language.

In a somewhat similar way, L. M. O'Toole's contribution concerns a semiotic system that is closely related to language, but is not the code of language itself, as this is usually conceived. His paper concerns a particular genre of *discourse*—as indeed do those of Halliday and Regan—but here the genre is written rather than oral. O'Toole presents and compares two contrasting models for the analysis and interpretation of fictional narrative: an analytic model that he has used for some time in the interpretation of Russian short stories, and

a generative model proposed by the Russians Zholkovsky and Scheg-
lov. He emphasizes, among other things, the patterns of relations
between the social roles and functions of the dramatis personae and
the linguistic devices used by the author in characterizing them, and
he concludes with an evaluation of the two models.

The semiotic system that is the object of study in Donald Preziosi's
contribution is, on the other hand, quite unrelated to language—
except that it is another semiotic system. He draws on the concepts
and notation of stratificational-relational grammar to describe the
relations between human beings, their culture and the semiotic
system that is realized in the spatial structures that we surround
ourselves with. In so doing, he demonstrates the use of relational
network analysis for the study of architectural form, and concludes
that 'it remains a reasonable assumption . . . that common cognitive
operations underlie' the deep semantic organizations of both language and architecture.

Before leaving Part II, it may be of interest to mention that, while
Preziosi's paper illustrates the application of stratificational-relational
grammar to a semiotic system that is very different from language,
there are also examples of the application of a systemic approach to
non-linguistic codes. One such is Terry Winograd's (1968/81) systemic study of (Western classical) music.

The question of the nature of the relationship between language
and culture hovers in the background, as it were, of most of the contributions to Parts I and II. But the three extended papers in Part III
stand out from the others in that all three are specifically addressed
to this question. Each of the three offers a general scheme for the
study of semiotics, each based upon a somewhat different approach
from the other two.

Sydney Lamb explores the possibility of extending the relational
network theory of stratificational grammar to a general relational
semiotics. Lamb gives Saussure's concept of the 'sign' a relational
network definition, and then uses it to explore the concept that the
structure of a culture is a network of relations. He thus presents
the hypothesis that 'the relation between language and culture can
be considered as a relation between two (possibly intertwined)
semiotic systems' in the strongest form to be encountered in this
book. A notable feature of the paper is the breadth of the variety
of examples given to support this view. In an approach such as
Lamb's, in which the emphasis is on relationships rather than
entities, the question arises of how the relational network relates
out to non-semiotic phenomena; how the mental (since Lamb's
is a cognitive model) relates out to the physical. There has long

been an answer at the 'phonetic' end of the language—in principle, that is: phonologists and phoneticians are in practice still far from agreement about the nature of the phonetics-phonology interface. But at the other end of language matters are even more difficult; it might for some be arguable that 'concepts' are non-semiotic, but concepts are certainly not part of the physical world. Here Lamb comes up with a bold new proposal to justify his strong adherence to the concept that semiosis is purely relational.

In his ambitiously titled 'Prolegomena to an understanding of semiotics and culture', Ashok R. Kelkar draws more heavily on philosophy than do the other contributors, to present a 'cosmology', as one might term it, that is lengthy (despite being most economically written) and highly structured. Its scope is extraordinary, and Kelkar locates in his overall framework—and so relates to each other— many of the main concepts of semiotics and linguistics, as well as the worlds of **gnosis** (cognition, insight), **aesthesis** (appreciation, evaluation), **praxis** (work, play), **poesis** (production, creation) and **cathexis** (love, loyalty). One of the pleasures of reading it is the incorporation of an aspect of Indian expository discourse: at regular intervals there are **sutras** that recapitulate the preceding section.

In the final paper Robin P. Fawcett presents an overall cognitive model of *language* (together with the other codes and semiotic systems) and *culture* (together with other aspects of the 'knowledge of the universe'). As with Lamb, there is a strong emphasis on modelling semiotic systems as relationships. But here there is also an equal emphasis on the complementary concept that a semiotic system is a *procedure* or, in the computing metaphor, a *program* for behaving. This leads him, in contrast with Lamb, to make a prime distinction between semiotic systems and the 'knowledge' that we draw upon in choosing between options at the semantic stratum in such a system—while not venturing a committed position on the ways in which that knowledge is stored. Thus, Fawcett's model does not preclude the possibility that some knowledge at least is stored in the way proposed by Lamb. Fawcett's emphasis, however, is less on how cultural knowledge is *stored* than on how it is *used*, in relation to system networks. Fawcett, like Halliday, is a systemicist, and the prime characteristic of systemic linguistics is that it gives a central place to the concept of choice between alternative meanings in social contexts. This paper introduces some key systemic concepts, illustrating these with a fragment from the grammar of English. Fawcett then makes the proposal that the systemic mode of modelling language should be extended to other semiotic systems, and offers a taxonomy of such systems. He next distinguishes culture from other aspects of 'knowledge of the universe', and illustrates the working relationship between language and culture, together with other aspects of the social context, through a detailed example. The paper concludes with a number of brief comparisons between Fawcett's own approach and the contributions to this book of Halliday, Watt, Lamb, and Kelkar.

One notable name was missing from the first section of this introduction—that of Saussure. Yet he is often referred to—and with justification—as the father of modern linguistics and, with Peirce, of semiotics. It can be argued, however, that most linguists and most semioticians have not paid sufficient attention to his emphasis on the interdependence of the two. One highly relevant piece of advice (directed in this case to linguists) is as follows:

If we are to discover the true nature of language, we must learn what it has in common with other semiological systems. [Saussure 1916/74: 17.]

Perhaps we can agree that a stereotypical sign system consists of choices between contrasting 'meanings' which are realized in contrasting 'forms'; and that, while many signs have only very simple internal syntax, language is well towards the complex end of the continuum between simple and complex syntax. This last fact is no doubt part of the reason why, over the past few decades, much of the work in linguistics has focused on problems in formal syntagmatic relations. Some linguists might argue that the relatively peripheral status given to paradigmatic as opposed to syntagmatic relations in standard transformational theory and its successors reflects the intrinsic nature of human language. But in that case one would like to be told why we tolerate all these complex contrasting structures, if it is not to realize complex contrasting meanings —and this brings us back to the missing statements on paradigmatic relations. It may therefore be useful to point out that most contributors to these volumes are distinguished by the fact that, in one way or another, they give equal weight to these paradigmatic relations of choice: to what might have been, but isn't, as well as to what is. In this they point a possible way forward for both their fellow linguists and for other semioticians.

We saw earlier how semiotic(s) has been defined by Locke and by Mead. It is instructive to see how it is defined in the new 1982 edition of *The Concise Oxford Dictionary* (COD). It is defined as a 'branch of linguistics concerned with signs and symbols'. This seems a somewhat odd definition in at least two ways. First, most modern scholars would surely recognize that semiotics must be concerned less with individual signs (or symbols) than with *sign systems*. A semiotic unit only has 'value', as Saussure emphasized, in terms of what we would today call its paradigmatic, syntagmatic and realizational relations with other semiotic units. And yet, although it has been fully explicit since Hjelmslev (1943/61) that the semiotician's task is to study not just signs but sign systems (i.e. grammars), introductory textbooks on semiotics still place excessive emphasis on the individual sign. Admittedly, it is an understandable tendency, since it is easier to comprehend a single instance of a sign than the abstract potential of a whole sign system, but if semiotics is to develop into a mature subject such issues must be faced. Perhaps the problem is that we lack sufficient grammars of semiotic systems other than language? If so, the next step is obvious: we need more grammars, and several contributors to this book discuss or illustrate ways of doing this.

It could also be argued that a major weakness in much of the current semiotics literature is that many semioticians seem to be simply unaware of developments in modern linguistics other than transformational generative grammar. Yet semioticians will certainly find useful many of the concepts of stratificational-relational grammar (Lamb 1966, 1970/73 and in this book, Lockwood 1972, Makkai and Lockwood 1973, and Preziosi's paper in this book). And semioticians of music and other semiotic systems are already putting to use concepts drawn from systemic theory (which is essentially complementary to, rather than a rival of, stratificational-relational grammar), such as the concept that the heart of the model consists of networks of choices between 'meaning' options, and the concept of functional components (Halliday, 1970, 1973, etc., Berry 1975, Fawcett 1980, Halliday and Martin 1981 and Halliday and Fawcett (to appear)).

The second and greater oddity in the COD's definition of semiotics lies in its assertion that semiotics is a branch of linguistics. This is, of course, a reversal of the true relationship; logically, since languages are just one class among myriads of classes of semiotic systems, linguistics is a branch of semiotics. Yet the COD definition contains a grain of truth, both because semioticians have traditionally drawn on linguistics for their basic concepts, and because there are incomparably more scholars whose central business is language than there are for all the rest of the sign systems put together.

The ideas we have been considering raise a number of issues for those who would at present call themselves either linguists or semioticians. The Society of Friends (Quakers) has a little booklet called *Advices and Queries*, and every now and then one will be read aloud in a meeting. Three 'queries' constructed on that model that linguists and semioticians might usefully put to themselves in the mid-1980s are these:

1 (to linguists) In view of the guiding principle proposed by Saussure that was cited above, have you set your study of language in the framework of the study of semiotic systems in general, so that, through realizing what language has in common with other semio-logical systems, you may distinguish its essential from its merely contingent characteristics, and so 'discover the true nature of language'?

2 (to semioticians) Have you relied too much on the early concepts in linguistics of Saussure, perhaps seasoned by Jakobson and supplemented by the initially attractive but now largely discarded Harris-Chomsky notion of the transformation, and have you con-sequently failed to draw adequately upon the relational network models of systemic and stratificational–relational grammar, as vital sources of linguistic concepts that may be relevant to the explica-tion of other semiotic systems?

3 (to both) Given that at present linguists typically function as a separate, though numerically overwhelming, sub-group within the wider family of semioticians, and given that most of the frag-mented scattering of other semioticians are left studying the various other sign systems as best they can, with academic attach-ments to departments where their work is often regarded as peri-pheral and eccentric rather than the crucial contribution to the study of man that it in fact is, has the time now come to press for the creation of more research centres and departments of Linguistics and Semiotics and/or of (Human) Communication (Studies)—as has already happened at, among others, Indiana University, USA, Rice University (Houston, USA), Murdoch University (Perth, Australia) and several polytechnics in Britain?

If the 1970s were the decade of 'social man', perhaps we should now, in this age of the explosion of information technology, begin to prepare for the 1990s to be the decade of 'semiotic man'. Indeed, it may well be that semiotics, with its strong humanistic tradition, has an important role to play in ensuring that we make the machines (and their programs) fit man, rather than man having to fit the machines.

Robin P. Fawcett
M. A. K. Halliday
Sydney M. Lamb
Adam Makkai

BIBLIOGRAPHY

Berry, M. (1975), *Introduction to Systemic Linguistics*, London, Batsford.

Copeland, J. E. (ed.) (1984), *New Directions in Linguistics and Semiotics*, Houston, Rice University Studies and Amsterdam, John Benjamins BV.

Fawcett, R. P. (1980), *Cognitive Linguistics and Social Interaction: Towards an Integrated Model of a Systemic Functional Grammar and the Other Components of a Communicating Mind*, Heidelberg, Julius Groos & Exeter University.

Fawcett, R. P. (1983), 'Language as a semiological system: a re-interpretation of Saussure', Invited Lecture to the Linguistics Association of Canada and the United States 1982, in Morreall (1983).

Garvin, P. (ed.) (1970), *Cognition: A Multiple View*, New York, Spartan.

Halliday, M. A. K. (1970), 'Language structure and language function', in Lyons (1970: 140-65).

Halliday, M. A. K. (1978), *Language as Social Semiotic*, London, Edward Arnold.

Halliday, M. A. K., and Fawcett, R. P. (eds) (to appear), *New Developments in Systemic Linguistics*, London, Batsford.

Halliday, M. A. K., and Martin, J. R. (eds) (1981), *Readings in Systemic Linguistics, 1956-1974*, London, Batsford.

Hjelmslev, L. (1943-61), *Prolegomena to a Theory of Language*, revised English edition, tr. Francis J. Whitfield, Madison, University of Wisconsin Press (original Danish version 1943.)

Lamb, S. M. (1966), *Outline of Stratificational Grammar*, Washington, D.C., Georgetown University Press.

Lamb, S. M. (1970-3), 'Linguistic and cognitive networks', in Garvin (1970) and in Makkai and Lockwood (1973).

Lockwood, D. G. (1972), *Introduction to Stratificational Linguistics*, New York, Harcourt, Brace and Jovanovich.

Lyons, J. (1970), *New Horizons in Linguistics*, Harmondsworth, Penguin.

Makkai, A., and Lockwood, D. G., (eds) (1973) *Readings in Stratificational Linguistics*, University; University of Alabama Press.

Morreall, J., (ed.) (1983), *The Ninth LACUS Forumm 1982*, Columbia, Hornbeam Press.

Saussure, F. de (1916/74), *Course in General Linguistics*, English edition tr. W. Baskin, London, Fontana (original French version 1916).

Sebeok, T. A., *et al.*, (eds) (1964), *Approaches to semiotics*, The Hague, Mouton.

Watt, W. C. (1975), 'What is the proper characterization of the alphabet? I: Desiderata' in *Visible Language*, 9, 293-327.

Watt, W. C. (1980), 'What is the proper characterisation of the alphabet? II: Composition' in *Ars Semiotica III*, 1, 13-46.

Watt, W. C. (1981), 'What is the proper characterisation of the alphabet? III: Appearance' in *Ars Semiotica IV*, 3, 269-313.

Winograd, T. (1968/81), 'Linguistics and the computer analysis of tonal harmony', *Journal of music theory*, 21, 1968 (2-49, 6-22, 42-3, 49-5) and in Halliday and Martin 1981.

Part I
Language as Social Semiotic

1 Language as code and language as behaviour: a systemic-functional interpretation of the nature and ontogenesis of dialogue

M. A. K. Halliday
University of Sydney, Australia

1.1 CODE AND BEHAVIOUR

A few years ago it was commonplace for articles on language 'behaviour' to begin with a disparaging reference to the fact that linguists confine their attention to the language 'code'; and this limitation was accepted as a fact of life, rather than being seen for what it was—a phenomenon arising at a particular time and place in the history of the study of language, when 'code' and 'behaviour' had been rigorously held apart. In the past ten years the two have been quietly merging again, and this has revitalized the concept of 'linguistics': the justification for having a discipline devoted to the study of an object 'language' is that only in such a context is the object seen simultaneously as system and as process.

The search for a unified 'code-and-behaviour' linguistics is not the same thing as the quest for a **linguistique de la parole**, or 'theory of performance', which is what the earlier formulations were often taken to imply; the two are in fact opposed. A theory of performance implies accepting the separation of code from behaviour, and then going on to study behaviour as if it was unrelated to any code. There was considerable misunderstanding on this issue, arising from the commitment of philosophical grammarians to a conceptual framework of the 'competence–performance' type, by reference to which any attention to what people actually say (let alone any attempt to predict what they will say) is outside the scope of linguistics altogether; cp. Lyons' 1968 remark that 'linguistic theory, at the present time at least, is not, and cannot be, concerned with the production and understanding of utterances in their actual situations of use'.

Philosophical grammar can be defined as the study of the code in isolation from behaviour: the attempt to explain the system without having regard to its use. This approach to language can be traced back at least to the ideas of the Modistae; it evolved through the rationalist grammars of the period following the Renaissance, and found vigorous expression in the transformation theory and other formal grammars of today. A philosopher of language is, by design, a purist, one whose conception of language demands a polarization between the ideal and the actual; this allows him to confine his linguistic pursuits to the study of the ideal, since anything too far removed from this is intractable to the very rigorous demands of his own conception of a theory. If such an attitude becomes dominant in linguistic circles, sooner or later it is likely to provoke a reaction from inside; and this may quite naturally take the form of a demand for a systematic study of the actual—for a so-called 'theory of performance'. Such a move appears at the time as revolutionary, but in fact it is reactionary, because it means accepting in full the rigid opposition between the pure and the contaminated which is just the cause of all the trouble. The line that is taken is: we admit the doctrine of purity, according to which what we are studying is defined as impure; but we want to study it anyway.

In this respect, philosophical grammars contrast with ethnographic or descriptive grammars, which tend to minimize the gap between the ideal and the actual. This latter tradition has its origins in classical linguistic theory, with its orientation towards the text (towards 'auctores' rather than 'artes', in the terms of the medieval metaphor); it continues in the empiricist writings of the seventeenth and eighteenth centuries, and is represented in modern times by the work of Boas and Sapir, the Prague school, Malinowski and Firth, and in the glossematic theories of Hjelmslev and Uldall. Ethnographic linguistics lacks the concept of purity; it does not set up any opposition between the system and its use, but instead attempts to handle code and behaviour under a single rubric.

Whereas the limiting case of a philosophical grammar is a logical syntax (i.e. an artificial language—hence philosophical grammarians tend to refer to language as 'natural language'), the limiting case of an ethnographic grammar is an **explication de texte** (an interpretative commentary on a single highly-valued instance of language use). Both are pre-eminently theoretical pursuits; there is no justification for denying the status of a 'theory' to anything that is not representable in a formal system.

These two perspectives, the logical–philosophical and the ethnographic–descriptive, are not really impossible to reconcile with one another. But from time to time in the history of linguistics they drift exaggeratedly apart, and so come to be counterposed; and this is what happened in the mid-twentieth century, leading to an almost total breakdown of communication between the two. This was no doubt partly because of a major breakthrough on the logical front, when Chomsky showed that it was possible to formalize the (American) structuralist interpretation of 'natural' language; but it had already been happening in the preceding decades, since the central goal of American structuralism was itself essentially a logico-philosophical one, namely the search for a formal theory of language as code—the readiness with which structuralists took up transformation theory suggests that they recognized this identity of goals. By the same token, the structuralist preoccupation with the formal properties of the code, and concomitant orientation away from a concern with behaviour, was at variance with the implicit goals of other groups of linguists, especially in Europe, who were attempting to account for both code and behaviour within a single theory. A good example of this is Hjelmslev, who attempted a systematic interpretation of the code within a conceptual framework in which code and behaviour are inseparable (as system and process) —an attempt that is still widely misunderstood despite Lamb's admirable exegesis (Lamb 1966).

Since it became clear that the idealized picture of language that is so successfully represented in formal terms involves excessive reduction, steps have been taken towards bringing the study of language as behaviour within the compass of philosophical linguistics. People talk; what is more, they talk to each other; and a linguistic theory which ignores these facts ends up by painting itself into a corner. The development of speech act theory was a move on the part of philosophical linguists towards taking them into account. The elaboration of the concept of 'communicative competence' was a comparable step taken from another angle, an attempt to explain behaviour as if it was a distinct *part of* the code. What this implies is that there are two kinds of knowledge, knowledge of the system and knowledge of its use, and that the two together make up the sum total of idealized linguistic competence.

The organizing concept of contemporary logico-philosophical linguistics is that of the 'rule'. The code is represented in terms of rules of grammar; and where the focus shifts on to behaviour, the rule leaps over the gap and we have rules of interpretation and rules of use. Ethnographic theories, on the other hand, tend to interpret language not as rules but as resource. The 'code' is a system, a potential; 'behaviour' is the actualization of that potential in real life situations; in other words, 'code' equals 'potential for behaviour'. For this reason the system is represented not as sets of rules but as networks of relations. The things people actually say are not seen as departures from a system of rules, randomly distorted or governed by their own special kinds of constraint; they are products of a system of relations, and the linguist's representation of the system is judged, relatively, more by its capacity to account for what people actually say (and write) and less by its internal consistency and elegance. Hence there are differences in the way spontaneous dialogue is interpreted in the two traditions. In speech act theory, a class of speech acts is treated as a theoretical construct *sui generis* (like a sentence in the grammar) and described as a 'structure', or set of rules, in terms of the logical presuppositions that speaker and hearer must share in order for the act to be interpreted as intended. In systemic theory the process of dialogue is treated as a shared potential and described as a 'system', or network of choices, in terms of the role relationships set up by the speaker for himself and the hearer and the encoding of these in the semantics of language.

In their representation of the grammatical system, philosophical and ethnographic theories can be contrasted in respect of what they do when the notion of constituent structure no longer gives results. As an organizing concept, in grammar, the part–whole relationship which linguists know as 'constituency' will take us so far (we owe to Zellig Harris a rather clear conception of just how far) and no further. It then breaks down. The transformational answer to this problem was to introduce more layers of constituent structure, of an increasingly abstract kind, and special rules for deriving one from another. The stratificational and systemic answer was to underpin the notion of constituency with relations of another kind. This reflects the fact that these latter theories are not, in essence, theories of linguistic *structure*. They are theories about what people can mean, and how they do it.

A systemic description is an attempt to interpret simultaneously both what language 'is' and what language 'does' (or, more realistically, what people do with it). It is characteristic of such an interpretation that it contains no such concept as 'the description of a sentence'. A sentence can, of course, be 'described' in terms of its grammatical structure; but this is merely an account of (part of) the means whereby it is realized. Describing a sentence, or describing any other linguistic item, in systemic theory means specifying the systems from which that item is derived—that is, the choices that are embodied in it (Halliday and Martin 1981). There is no way in which a structure is first described and then by a separate step brought into paradigmatic relation with other structures. A 'description' is a statement of paradigmatic relationships—in the terms used above, it is a characterization of language as a resource.

A related feature of systemic theory is the conception of a 'natural' grammar: the view that linguistic form is to be explained as the reflex of linguistic function. The form of the code, in other words, has been determined in the course of linguistic evolution by the patterns of its use, so that the system is organized internally on a functional basis. This provides the principle behind the interpretation of grammatical structure in functional terms; not only (1) that grammatical functions like Agent, Process, Goal, and also Theme, Subject, Complement and the rest express systematic options in meaning but also (2) that the different components in the grammar (e.g. transitivity, mood, and theme in the grammar of the clause) are structured in ways which derive naturally from the 'metafunctional' components of the semantic system (cp. Halliday 1979b).

In stressing the interpenetration of code and behaviour, therefore, we are not simply concerned with explaining behaviour in terms of the code. More significant, in the longer term, is the aim of explaining the code in terms of behaviour. The system is determined by the process. It is this perspective that is implied by the notion of a 'functional' theory of language.

1.2 CONTEXT, PREDICTION, AND CHOICE

By narrowing the gap between language as code and language as behaviour, and using each to explain the other, we come closer to interpreting language in relation to its place in people's lives. Language is once more back in its social context. For those for whom linguistics always had this wider perspective, it is refreshing to find the ideas of earlier 'socio'-linguists like Firth being taken up again and serving as a point of departure for new developments and insights. Firth did not, of course, call what he was doing 'sociolinguistics'; for him, it was simply linguistics. The 'socio' prefix was introduced after his time to avoid a confrontation with the prevailing ideology; but it always had a rather apologetic air, and can now be thankfully abandoned or reserved for studies which genuinely involve both linguistic and social theory.

Our conception of the social context of language will depend, naturally, on our conception of language itself. If code and behaviour are divorced, then it is only the behaviour that *has* a social context; in that case, social context means no more than 'situation of the utterance', the non-verbal particulars that surround and provide the

environment for a particular verbal event. But when code and behaviour are married, the notion of social context is very different,
because it includes not only the social context of the behaviour
(Malinowski's 'context of situation') but also the social context of
the code (Malinowski's 'context of culture').

The social context of the linguistic code is the culture. But in
order to refer to this we need to represent the culture as an information system, or rather as a network of information systems: that is,
in semiotic terms. A culture is a configuration of semiotic systems;
the central problem is to interpret language in a way which enables
us to relate it to other semiotic processes.

The social context of language behaviour—the situation in which
meanings are exchanged—is also a semiotic construct; and it is
perceived as such by those taking part. The interactants in a speech
situation treat that situation as embodying aspects of the social
order—as having a certain potential in terms of which their own
acts of meaning will be interpreted and valued. They have to do this
in order to be able to make predictions about the meanings which
are likely to be exchanged. There is nothing mysterious about the
notion of predicting what people are going to say. We do it all the
time; if we did not do so, we should never be able to understand
each other, since understanding depends on having a good idea of
what is coming next. The social context of any conversation is con-
tinuously being created and modified, by the course of the conversation itself as well as by other processes that may be taking place; and
those involved unconsciously assess its ongoing semiotic potential,
using this information not only to interpret the meanings of others
but also to project the likely scope and interpretation of their own
subsequent acts of meaning.

What we do, in other words, is to make sensible guesses about
how those involved in the exchange of meanings are going to draw
on the overall resources of the linguistic system. These guesses are
of two interrelated kinds: generic and textual.

1. In the first place we make guesses about the genre, or 'register',
which is involved. The register is the *functional variety*, the con-
figurations and combinations of choices of meaning which make up
a recognizable semantic domain. As adults, we tend to have a rather
well-formed sense of register, an awareness of the semantic design
of any given social context, and of the areas of meaning that are
likely to be explored. How much we depend on this awareness
becomes clear when we try to interact in a foreign culture; even
though we 'know the language', we may be quite wrong in our interpretation of what meanings the context demands. It is beyond the

scope of this chapter to discuss which features of the social context seem to determine which of the different kinds of meaning; I have written about this elsewhere (Halliday 1978), suggesting a systematic link between the semiotic structure of contexts and the functional components of the semantic system.

2. In the second place we make guesses about the 'texture', the kinds of cohesion and organization of information that are involved. We have a good idea, in any given context, how much new information is likely to be presented in a typical semantic or grammatical unit (e.g. in one 'turn', or in one clause); what form this new information will take; how each part of the discourse is likely to link up with what has gone before, and so on. This is closely bound up with our awareness of register, because the texture is in fact one aspect of the register, being largely determined by the semiotic mode, the particular part that the text is playing in the given context of situation.

Exchanges of meaning succeed, if they do (and it is remarkable how often they do succeed), because each of those taking part has some idea of what the others will mean and assumes that they have some idea of what he will mean. As speakers and listeners, we project the linguistic system on to the social system (this is, after all, how each of us constructed the linguistic system in the first place), interpreting verbal meanings as the expression of the meanings that are inherent in the culture. Any construct of cultural meanings—that is, any social context—is realized in the form of acts of meaning in the various semiotic modes of which language is one. The ongoing processes of linguistic choice, whereby a speaker is selecting within the resources of the linguistic system, are effectively cultural choices, and acts of meaning are cultural acts. We are, no doubt, 'free' to mean as we choose—and culture can be defined as how far our freedom of meaning is constrained, the extent to which people's acts of meaning depart from this idealized randomness.

In a systemic representation of language, the basic organizing concept is that of choice. A choice has two components: it consists of (1) a set of 'things', of which one must be chosen; and (2) an entry condition—the environment in which the choice is made. The environment of a choice could be thought of as a structural setting or background; but it can equally be represented as the combined outcome of a range of other choices. So meanings are represented as networks of choices. The formal representation of a choice is called (following Firth) a 'system'; hence, a choice network is a system network. The description of a language takes the form of system networks.[1]

All three levels of the linguistic system, semantic, lexicogram-matical, and phonological, are interpreted in this way as system networks. The concept of 'choice', however, has a different signifi-cance at each level.

The exchange of meanings is an ongoing process of contextualized choice. An act of meaning in language is a process of semantic choice. Choices at other levels, lexicogrammatical and phonological, tend to be predetermined, because they serve as the realization of choices in the semantic system—although there are 'de-automatized' choices at other levels, for example the choice of parallel grammatical structures, or of syllables which rhyme. But semantic choices are also, in the final analysis, the 'realization' of choices at some higher level, somewhere in the semiotic systems of the culture. If they were not, it would scarcely be possible for ordinary spontaneous con-versation to have the magical power that it has, the power of con-structing and organizing social situations, of providing a foundation for interpersonal relations and the socialization process, of main-taining and giving a history to personal identity, and of creating and modifying the structure of reality. At the same time, it must be borne in mind that once a particular symbolic system comes into being, engendered by the culture, it takes on an independent exist-ence and so engenders meanings of its own, meanings which become part of the culture in their turn; and language is the paradigm example of this process. Forcing, threatening, and making contact with a person are non-semantic acts, which may or may not be realized semantically through language; ordering, warning, and greet-ing are semantic acts—which thereby become part of the cultural semiotic and take on social value. In like manner, building a shelter is a non-semantic act, one which happens to be subject to certain natural laws; whereas encoding this process in a transitivity structure is a semantic act—through which a model of transitivity then be-comes part of the culture.

In order to illustrate the notion of semantic choice, in a functional theory of language as we understand this concept (a social-semiotic, 'system-and-process' interpretation), we have to relate some portion of the language code to language behaviour, and both to some higher-level order of meaning. We shall try to do this briefly by considering the nature of dialogue in very general terms. The pro-cedure will be (1) to represent the elementary relations of dialogue in a hierarchy of three networks, (a) social-contextual, (b) semantic, and (c) grammatical, showing how each can be interpreted as a re-coding of the one above; (2) to present and comment on short passages of recorded spontaneous conversation in the light of these, showing what kinds of extension of the elementary picture are necessary to the interpretation of typical instances; and (3) to give an account of the ontogeny of dialogue as it appeared in the developmental history of a particular child.

At the social-contextual level, the dynamic of dialogue consists in assigning, taking on, and carrying out a variety of interaction roles. These roles are themselves defined by a small number of very general semiotic processes, and it is these that we shall take as our point of departure. The choices that are open to a speaker within this range of interpersonal options are then coded in the semantic system, as 'speech functions' of statement, question and the like; and these in turn are recoded in the grammatical system, as categories of mood. The coding is not one to one; there are many departures from a simple bi-unique relationship. But these are not, in general, the arbitrary patterns of neutralization and diversification that are found at the lower levels of the system. Rather they are systematic restructurings which serve to build flexibility into the system, and allow speakers to introduce infinite variety into the tenor of their microsemiotic encounters.

1.3 A MODEL OF DIALOGUE

In the most general terms, at the level of social context, dialogue can be interpreted as a process of exchange. It is an exchange involving two variables: (1) the nature of the commodity that is being exchanged, and (2) the roles that are defined by the exchange process.

1. The commodity may be either (a) goods-&-services or (b) information (cp. Ervin-Tripp 1964). In **Give me a Herald, please!** or **Let me fix it for you!**, what is being exchanged is goods-&-services, and language is functioning simply as a means of furthering the exchange. On the other hand, in **Is it cold outside?** or **I met Colin today**, what is being exchanged is information, and language is both the means of exchange and the manifestation of the commodity being exchanged.

The distinction between information and goods-&-services is theoretically a very fundamental one, despite the fact that there will be many tokens—actual speech events—of an intermediate or a complex kind. Unlike goods-&-services, which are non-verbal commodities, information is a 'commodity' which is brought into being only through language (or perhaps other semiotic systems). In the case of goods-&-services, the exchange of symbols helps to *bring about* the exchange; but the two are distinct processes, the one a means to the other. In the case of information, on the other hand, the exchange of symbols actually *constitutes* the exchange; there is only one process, and we are simply looking at two aspects of it—the intention, and the manifestation.

2. The role of a speaker taking part in the exchange may be one of either (a) giving or (b) demanding. He may be giving information (**I met Colin today.**), or giving goods-&-services (**Let me fix it for you!**); or demanding information (**Is it cold outside?**), or demanding goods-&-services (**Give me a Herald, please!**).

When the speaker takes on a role of giving or demanding, by the same token he assigns a complementary role to the person he is addressing. If I am giving, you are called on to accept; if I am demanding, you are called on to give. There are (a) exchange-initiating roles, those taken on by the speaker himself, and (b) responding roles, those assigned by the speaker to the addressee and taken on by the addressee when he becomes the speaker in his turn. We can take account of this and represent the system for one move as in Figure 1.1.

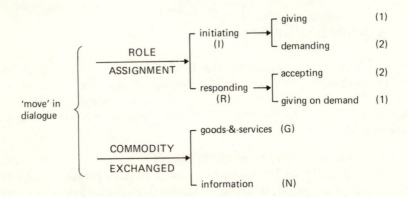

Fig. 1.1 The system of dialogue (a): level of social context—the 'move'

In Figure 1.1, dialogue is being represented at a level that is 'above' the linguistic code: we are interpreting it as a system of the social context. The system network expresses the potential that inheres in one move in the dynamics of personal interaction. When we consider dialogue in this way, as a form of the exchange of social meanings, we are looking at it as a semiotic process, and therefore as one that is in principle capable of being realized through systems other than language. To the extent that other semiotic systems have the facility for encoding the two components of the process (the assignment of roles in the exchange and the nature of the exchange itself), to that extent they can replace language as 'carriers' of dialogue. If no other semiotic systems display these two properties, this will be an instance of a social process that specifically requires language for its realization. This does not mean, of course, that we should therefore not interpret it in terms of the social context: even where a particular function is served only by language, we still seek to explain that function in terms of the social semiotic, and in this way show how it relates to other semiotic processes in which systems other than language do operate as variants (e.g. exchange of greetings).

The next step in the interpretation is to move into the linguistic system, at the 'highest' level, the level of semantics; and to show the network of semantic options by which the options in the exchange process are encoded as meanings in language. This will be Lamb's 'sememic' stratum. At this level are introduced concepts of the kind traditionally referred to as 'speech functions': statement, question, and the like. However, the set of such speech functions that will typically be found in grammar books, namely statement, question, command, and exclamation, is one that is wholly derived from the grammatical system, the next level 'down' in the coding process; these terms are really semantic relabellings of categories previously defined by the mood system in the grammar. In other words, the interpretation faces only one way. If on the other hand the semantic system is being seen as a distinct level of coding that is intermediate between the grammar and the social context, the interpretation will face both ways. In this perspective, the categories of speech function are both (a) *realizing* the social-contextual options of role assignment and commodity exchanged and (b) *realized by* the grammatical options of mood—as well as (c) forming a coherent system in their own right. The basic system for the semantics of dialogue can be represented as in Figure 1.2.

Let us now try to show how these semantic options serve to encode the dynamic role-play of dialogue. For this, as for all realization

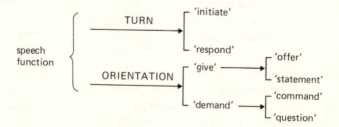

Fig. 1.2 The system of dialogue (b): level of semantics—the 'speech function'

statements, we shall need the concept of *congruence*. A 'congruent' realization is that one which can be regarded as typical—which will be selected in the absence of any good reason for selecting another one. This 'good reason' type of default principle is widely found in the interfacing of semiotic systems. Wherever there is one variant that is congruent, it is this variant that is likely to be taught as a 'rule' to foreign learners of a language when they are first presented with the feature in question. In real life, we rarely confine ourselves to congruent realizations for very long; not only because the resulting discourse easily becomes boring but also, and more significantly, because *many of the more delicate distinctions within any system depend for their expression on what in the first instance appear as non-congruent forms*. Nevertheless as speakers of a language we are aware of what is the congruent mode of encoding of any feature, and we use this as a kind of base line: for example, however rarely we may actually use an imperative in giving orders, we have a feeling that it is in some sense the unmarked way of doing so. By no means all linguistic features display a set of variant realizations such that one of them clearly stands out as congruent; but many do. Table 1.1 shows the patterns of congruence between the social-contextual system of moves in dialogue and the semantic system of speech functions.

Table 1.1 Semantic realization of categories of the social context
            (congruent pattern)

Move in dialogue:	Speech function by which typically encoded:
(I 1 G)	'initiate : offer'
(I 1 N)	'initiate : statement'
(I 2 G)	'initiate : command'
(I 2 N)	'initiate : question'
(R 2 G)	'respond (to offer) : accept (command in response)'
(R 2 N)	'respond (to statement) : acknowledge (question in response)'
(R 1 G)	'respond (to command) : comply (offer in response)'
(R 1 N)	'respond (to question) : answer (state in response)'

Note that the reciprocity of responses is typical not only of responses to demanding, where a command is responded to by an offer, and a question by a statement, but also of responses to giving: we frequently acknowledge an offer by giving a command, and acknowledge a statement by asking a question. Examples:

1. Give me a Herald, please! — Here!   'command +
                                                  compliance'
2. Let me fix it for you!   — Yes, do!   'offer + acceptance'
3. Is it cold outside?   — It is.   'question + answer'
4. I met Colin today.   — Did you?   'statement +
                                                acknowledgement'

Again, it should be stressed that these are examples of congruent patterns. As ways of expressing the exchange of roles in dialogue, they are typical, but in no sense obligatory.

The meanings are, in turn, coded as 'wordings': that is as selections of options in the lexicogrammatical system (Lamb's 'lexological' stratum). Let us represent this once again as a network, still keeping to the most general features of the system (see Figure 1.3).

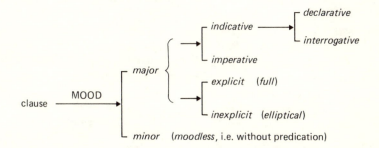

Fig. 1.3 The system of dialogue (c): level of lexicogrammar—the 'mood'

Table 1.2 shows how these grammatical features figure as (congruent) realizations of the semantic options. Table 1.3 summarizes the principal categories: situational, 'semantic', and *lexicogrammatical*.

Table 1.2 Lexicogrammatical realization of semantic categories
(congruent pattern)

Speech function:	Mood by which typically encoded:
'initiate'	*full*
'respond'	*elliptical* (or *minor*)
'offer'	(various; no congruent form)
'statement'	*declarative*
'command'	*imperative*
'question'	*interrogative*

Table 1.3 Summary of principal categories

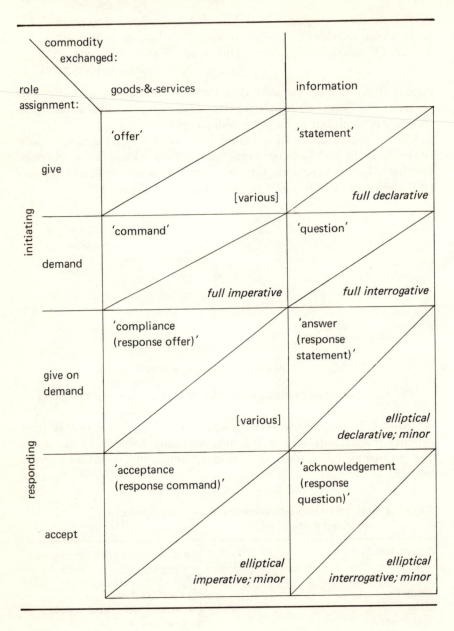

1.4 SOME EXAMPLES OF DIALOGUE BETWEEN PARENT AND CHILD

We have now set up a three-level interpretation of dialogue based on the principle of congruence, showing the exchange of meaning roles first coded as speech functions (as linguistic meanings of an interpersonal kind) and then recoded as grammatical features, as terms in the mood system. The next step is to ask: what kinds of extension of these patterns of congruence do we find in real life dialogue?

The system networks are, of course, idealized constructs; they are a representation of part of the code. However, in setting them up and relating them to each other through the concepts of 'coding' and 'congruence', we are not treating them as 'pure' categories from which instances of living speech are set off as deviant, as in some sort of competence-performance model. The idealization consists in the fact that up to this point the networks (a) have introduced only the most general (least 'delicate') distinctions, and (b) have been shown as related to each other only through their most typical (most 'congruent') realizations. When they are used in the interpretation of language behaviour they will need to be filled in and extended, so as to show incongruent patterns of relationship, and to introduce more delicate choices.

Let us now consider some examples from real life. Passage A is a dialogue between Nigel, at 1;10, and his mother:

Passage A

Nigel	Have blue pin all right!	(1)
Mother	The blue pin has got lost.	(2)
Nigel	Under béd?	(3)
Mother	No it's not under the bed.	(4)
Nigel	Blue pin got lòst. White pin got lost?	(5)
Mother	No the white pin didn't get lost.	(6)

In (3-4) and (5-6) we have something very close to an exchange of meanings that is congruent in both dimensions: both in terms of what follows what, and in terms of how each one is realized. Nigel demands information and his mother responds by giving it. This exchange is encoded semantically as: Nigel asks a question and his mother makes a statement which is an answer to it. Grammatically, the encoding on Nigel's part turns out to be congruent once we know what his system is at the time. At this stage, Nigel's primary opposition is one between 'response demanded' and 'response not demanded'.

This system is realized by intonation: falling tone realizes 're-sponse not demanded', rising tone realizes 'response demanded'. Hence what would in adult speech be questions and commands belong to a single semantic category of 'pragmatic' utterances realized by the rising intonation contour. His mother's responses are also grammatically congruent, with the proviso that in both instances she used the full and not the elliptical form of the clause.

In (1–2) we have a different situation. Here Nigel is demanding goods-&-services; this is again encoded congruently as a pragmatic utterance, with rising tone, being differentiated from a demand for information by the **have** plus **all right** (the grammatical distinction between command and question is not yet systematic in his language). His mother, however, gives a response that is incongruent: it is a statement, not an offer, and functions as a supplementary response, one which answers by implication: 'so you can't have it'. Here therefore the response network needs to be expanded to include features such as those in Figure 1.4 (cp. Halliday and Hasan 1976:207).

Fig. 1.4 Types of indirect response

The response in Nigel's mother's turn (2) brings out the fact that the only responses considered so far had been of the 'direct' kind. In real life, however, responses are very often indirect; there is no rule requiring a direct answer to a question. A good example of a disclaimer can be seen in this exchange between Nigel, at 4;11, and his father (Passage B):

Passage B

Nigel   Why does as plasticine gets longer it gets thinner?
Father   That's a very good question: why does it?
Nigel   Because more of it is getting used ùp.
Father   Well . . .
Nigel   Because more of it is getting used up to make it lònger, thàt's whý, and so it goes thinner.

His father's response simply ducks the question, and Nigel goes on to supply an answer for himself—a very appropriate one, as it happens.

Passage C shows the exchange of goods-&-services (offers and commands) taking place largely in minor clauses (Nigel at 3;2):

Passage C

Father   [playing a game called Grrr] One more grrr.
Nigel   No, thrèe more.
Father   All right. [They play one.] Now two more.
Nigel   [thinking he is being cheated] No—thrèe more.
Father   Yes, but we've had one of the three, so it's two more
          now. [Nigel accepts, unconvinced.]

Contrast this with Passage D, where the exchange of goods-&-services takes the form of major declarative clauses (Nigel at 3;3):

Passage D

Nigel   You can have the box car.
Father   But I don't want the box car; I want the diesel engine.
Nigel   I'm not going to give you the diesel engine.
Father   Then I'll have the box car.
Nigel   But I'm not going to give you one you don't want.

In Passage E (Nigel at 3;3), all instances are congruent throughout:

Passage E

Mother   Go and tell Daddy that lunch is ready!
Nigel   [knocking on study door] Lunch ready.
Father   Thank you!—I'm coming.
Nigel   Múmmy, is it reády, or is it stàrting to get ready?
Mother   It's ready.
Nigel   But it's not on the tăble.

Passages D and E illustrate a different point. Both can be interpreted in terms of the general concepts that we started with, without further elaboration; but whereas the realizations in Passage E are congruent (and it is useful to be reminded that congruent patterns do frequently occur!), those in Passage D involve incongruent realization at various points. In this connection it is worth remarking that, as a general feature, languages display a greater tendency to congruence in the exchange of information than in the exchange of goods-&-services. This is hardly surprising. Since information is a commodity that is defined and brought into being only by semiotic systems, with language leading the way, it is no surprise to find that there exist clearly defined categories of declarative and interrogative in the grammar, and that these are typically used as the mode of giving and demanding information. When it comes to exchanging goods-&-services, however, this is a process that takes place independently of the existence of a semiotic in which to encode it; and languages do not display clearcut categories in the grammar corresponding to offers and commands. The imperative is at best a fringe category, teetering between finite and non-finite (in languages which make this distinction), having either no distinct clause or verb form or else one that is only minimally distinguished; and even when a distinct imperative form does exist it may be rarely used, with other, non-congruent forms taking over the command function. The position is even clearer with offers: no language seems to have a clearly distinguished grammatical form for offers, the closest perhaps being special types of indicative like the English **shall I . . . ?**

This is not to say that offers and commands are not ordinarily verbalized at all. On the contrary, they often are. The difference between information and goods-&-services is that, since information is a semiotic commodity, it is impossible to exchange it except by a semiotic process—in fact a semiotic process can be defined as one through which information is exchanged; so when we exchange information, there are explicit and regular grammatical patterns for doing so, the forms of declarative and interrogative mood, and these are the forms that are typically used. Goods-&-services on the other hand can be exchanged without the intervention of any symbolic act. Adults, being oriented towards the verbal mode, do typically verbalize offers and commands: for example, **here you are!, would you like a newspaper?, shall I hold the door open for you?, come on—follow me!** But the grammatical system of English does not display any clearly defined pattern of congruence in the realization of offers and commands; and this is true of many other languages, perhaps all. The exchange of goods-&-services, because of its lesser dependence on language, has not brought about the evolution of special modes of expression in the same way that these have evolved for the exchange of information. We shall see in the next section that, in the course of developing the adult pattern of speech functions, Nigel did pass through a stage when he had a relatively clearcut semantic system of 'let me' (offer), 'let you' (command) and 'let you and me' (suggestion). But this regularity is lost in the adult language.

Passage F (Nigel at 6;5) illustrates a question–answer sequence where the response is direct (unlike those in B and C) but involves a modality:

Passage F

Nigel [looking at real estate section of newspaper] Look at that very very small print! . . . Do they always print as small as that in very big bóoks?

Father Not always, no—

Nigel [interrupts; looking at Father's typewriter, a large old-fashioned office machine not yet unpacked after removal] Wè've got a printing machine in òur house, hàven't we.

Father We've got a typewriter, yes.

Here, Nigel's father's second response is an indirect one; it answers by implication. His first response, on the other hand, is direct; but it is accompanied by a modality **not always**, echoing the **always** in Nigel's question. To take account of this we shall have to return to the notion of a question, realizing a demand for information, and consider the options open to the person to whom such a demand is addressed. So far we have spoken of dialogue as the assignment of roles by the speaker: the speaker adopts one role for himself, and imposes another complementary role on to the hearer. In fact, however, what he assigns to the hearer is not a role but a choice of roles. The hearer has considerable discretion in the way he chooses to play the part that is assigned to him. We could represent the choice for 'response to question' as in Figure 1.5. Note that the simple answer 'yes', or 'no', already involves a number of steps or choice points in the logical structure of the decision process.

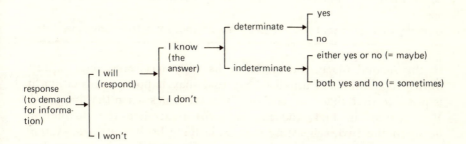

Fig. 1.5 Options open to respondent facing demand for information

The response **not always** in Passage F has the feature 'indeterminate'. An indeterminate response is one that is 'tagged' by the speaker with some assessment of its validity: it is true only with a certain likelihood, or only for a certain proportion of the time. This validity assessment is realized semantically as the system of modality; and there are two dimensions to this, (1) 'maybe', i.e. probability, and (2) 'sometimes', which we might refer to as 'usuality' (Figure 1.6).

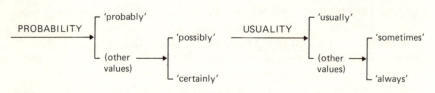

Fig. 1.6 Semantic systems of modality

Various considerations suggest that these two systems are semantically isomorphic. In the first place, in both of them there is a median value in which negation applies without change of meaning either to the modality or to the thesis, contrasting with two outer values in which the negation of one modality is equivalent to the other modality with negation of the thesis (Table 1.4):

Table 1.4 Median and outer values of modality

Probability	Usuality
probably (not so) = (not probably) so	usually (not so) = (not usually) so
but	but
possibly (not so) = (not certainly) so	sometimes (not so) = (not always) so
and	and
certainly (not so) = (not possibly) so	always (not so) = (not sometimes) so

In the second place, the modal verbs **will, may, must,** etc. express both probability and usuality: e.g. **that may happen** means either 'it is possible that that happens' or 'there are times when that happens'. Very often, in fact, the modal verbs neutralize the distinction between the two, suggesting that underlying both is a single system representing the degree of the speaker's commitment to the validity of the statement he is making (Figure 1.7). More delicately, the 'high'

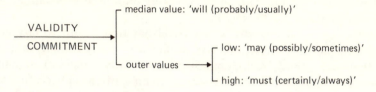

Fig. 1.7 Generalized system of validity commitment (modality)

value embodies a further systematic distinction into 'relatively high' ('should': almost certainly/nearly always) and 'absolutely high' ('must': certainly/always), which helps to explain negative adverbs like **hardly** (**hardly ever/hardly likely** = 'nearly always not'/'almost certainly not'). This does not figure in the present illustration.

Modality can be interpreted as an elaboration of the category 'indeterminate'. It is incorporated into the network as in Figure 1.8.

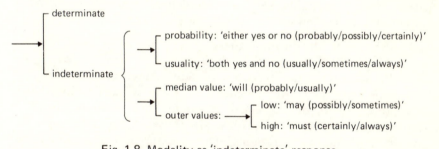

Fig. 1.8 Modality as 'indeterminate' response

Modals do, of course, appear in statements and questions which are not responses, though it could be argued that they are inherently associated with responding rather than initiating. In Passage F, Nigel's question already includes the usuality term **always** ('does this apply to all instances? I know that it applies to at least one'), and the response is both congruent and appropriate. Strictly speaking, in its context the response is not indeterminate, since given the question 'is this always so?' the response 'not always' is equivalent to a determinate 'no'; respondents however usually seem to repeat the modality in such instances, perhaps because they feel that a bare **No** might be interpreted as 'it is never so'.

1.5 THE ORIGINS OF DIALOGUE

In this section we give a brief sketch of how Nigel developed the system of dialogue, starting from the earliest stage of his protolanguage at 8 months old. For the fuller account on which this summary is based see Halliday 1975, 1979a.

At the age of 8 months, when Nigel has first begun to engage in systematic acts of meaning, the choice of speech function ('give me that', 'do that', etc.) constitutes the only range of semantic choice that is available to him: the signalling of the speech function takes up the entire meaning of the utterance. By the beginning of the third year, in the final stages of his transition to an adult-like system, the choice of speech function is becoming freely combinable (in principle—not all combinations will make sense) with all choices in ideational meaning. Nigel has worked his way up through a series of developmental steps to that highly complex point where, for example, the ideational meaning 'eat + toast' can be mapped on to any of the interpersonal meanings 'demand + goods-&-services' ('I want to eat toast'), 'give + information' ('I am eating toast'), and, incipiently, 'demand + information' ('are you eating toast?'); including various more delicate sub-categories. What is the route he has followed to reach this point?

1. At 0;8, when the protolanguage is just appearing, Nigel creates a system which offers a startlingly accurate preview of one of the most fundamental characteristics of adult language, the language he will one day take over (Figure 1.9). He now has developed five signs, three of them expressed gesturally and two vocally. The meanings he expresses by gesture are those in the active sphere: 'give me that' and 'do that for me'. The meanings he expresses by voice are those in the reflective sphere: 'let's be together' and 'that's interesting'. Nigel will shortly abandon the gestural mode almost entirely;

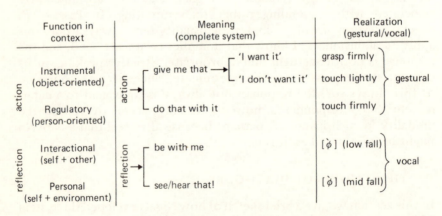

Fig. 1.9 Protolanguage, early (0;8)

meanwhile, for a brief five or six weeks he has anticipated what is the central functional distinction of the adult language, that between interpersonal meanings—language as action—which are typically expressed through structures of a prosodic, non-segmental kind, and ideational meanings—language as reflection—which are typically expressed through segmental, constituent-like structures, the sort that are appropriately represented by trees in a structural description.

2. From here on, and into his second year, Nigel moves on to construct, with the help of the adults around him (since they understand him, and respond with meanings of their own), a protolanguage which serves his four elementary functions: the instrumental, the regulatory, the interactional, and the personal (Figure 1.10). The last of these functions is 'self'-oriented; it is the expression of Nigel's own cognitive and affective response to his environment. The first three, however, are 'other'-oriented: and here Nigel distinguished almost from the start between initiating an exchange of meanings

Function in context	Meaning (partial system; complete system now has 29 distinct elements)		Realization (phonological)
Instrumental	give →	initiating 'I want that'	[nànànànà]
		responding → 'yes I want (object present)'	[yï]
		'yes I want (object or service mentioned)'	[â]
Regulatory	do →	initiating 'do that (again)'	[à], [ə̀]
		responding → 'yes (let's) do that'	[ɜ̀]
		'no don't (let's) do that'	[à̋ à̏]
Interactional	be with →	greeting (personalized)	[ama], [dada], [an:a]
		engagement → initiating 'let's look at this together'	[dɛ̀ə], [ādà]
		responding 'here I am'	[ɛ̀::] (breathy)
Personal	see/ like →	'I see/hear'	['dɔ̀]
		'I like'	[ɛᵛǐ:]

Fig. 1.10 Protolanguage, middle (1;0)

and responding to a meaning that is addressed to him—between, for example, 'give me that!' and 'yes I want that!'. The distinction between active and reflective functions is no longer significant: both kinds of meaning are there, but the systematic distinction between them is (for the time being) lost.

3. Next, at 15-16 months, Nigel begins to add content to these generalized meanings (Figure 1.11). The meaning is no longer just 'I want that', 'that's interesting', but 'I want the clock', 'that's interesting—a bus', and so on. He continues to use the generalized

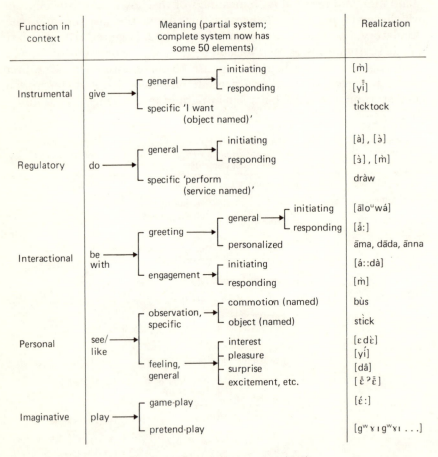

Fig. 1.11 Protolanguage, late (1;4)

Note: the general elements are still protolinguistic, realized phonologically as complexes of articulation and intonation; the specific elements are now names, and so encoded through the intermediary of the lexicogrammatical system. Realizations given in orthography are examples of the categories in question.

protolinguistic expressions alongside these new forms; in particular, baby signs expressing feelings persist well into the stage when he is already using words and structures.

4. At 19 months, Nigel reintroduces the active/reflective distinction in a new form; and it serves him as the principal strategy for the transition from protolanguage to language (Figure 1.12). The distinction is now encoded systematically: a rising tone means 'response demanded', and signals an utterance with a pragmatic function, e.g. **play chúffa** 'let's play with the train', **more grávy** 'I want more gravy' while a falling tone means 'no responses demanded'—the utterance has a 'mathetic' (learning, or reality-constructing) function, e.g. **red sweàter** 'that's my red sweater', **loud mùsic** 'that's a loud

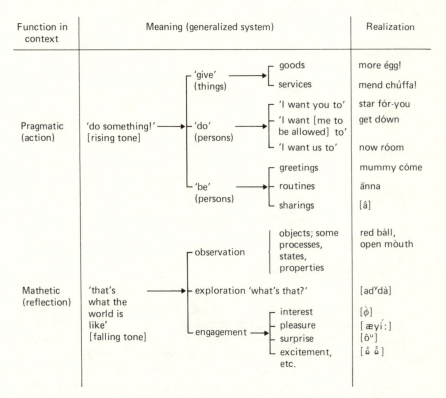

Fig. 1.12 Transition, early (1;7)

Note: The feature 'engagement' is still realized protolinguistically. Other meanings are realized lexicogrammatically, as words, with structures now beginning to appear (e.g. **Mummy come! Red ball.**); pragmatic on rising tone, mathetic on falling tone. Realizations given in orthography are examples of the categories in question.

piece of music'. Utterances in the mathetic function are self-sufficient; no action is called for. Utterances in the pragmatic function on the other hand carry the general meaning 'do something'——the person addressed is required to give a particular object or service, to engage in some kind of activity ('let you', 'let me', or 'let's') or to interact in some particular way.

5. By 22 months, the pragmatic category has extended to utterances which demand a verbal response; that is, to questions (Figure 1.13).

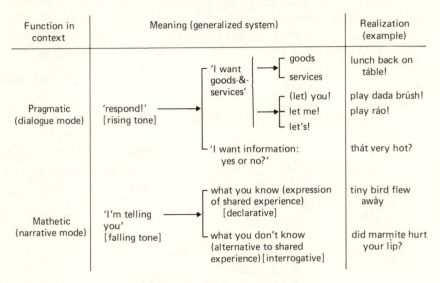

Fig. 1.13 Transition, late (1;10)

Note: All meanings are now realized lexicogrammatically, as words in structures; mathetic as indicative (declarative = 'you know this already', interrogative = 'you don't know this yet'), pragmatic as various imperative-like and minor clause structures.

The pragmatic feature 'do something' now means either 'provide goods-&-services' or 'provide information'. Hence all Nigel's questions, including WH-questions, have a rising tone. They do not, however, take the interrogative form. The interrogative, which Nigel now introduces into his system, serves instead to encode a new distinction within what was the mathetic function. The meaning of the mathetic has now evolved in the direction of 'I am giving information'; and Nigel develops a systematic distinction which has no counterpart in the adult language: a distinction between 'I'm telling you something which you know already' (i.e. you shared with me the experience I'm talking about——declarative) and 'I'm telling you

something which you don't know' (i.e. my talking about it serves as
an alternative to shared experience—interrogative). Hence only the
interrogative is strictly 'giving information', in the expected adult
sense of something that is not known to the person addressed.
Adults, of course, spend much of their time giving information that
is already known; but they do not recognize it as a systematic
category.

6. At the end of the second year, when Nigel is just on the threshold
of entry to the adult language, in the sense of being about to adopt
the functional semantic patterns of the mother tongue, he has introduced many more delicate distinctions; but the primary distinctions
he is making are now coming to approximate the speech functions of
the adult language (Figure 1.14). It is not difficult to see how this
evolves into the adult system as outlined in Section 1.3 above, based
on the exchange of meanings of the two kinds that we recognized
there: goods-&-services, where language is ancillary to a (non-
symbolic) process that itself is independent of language, and
information, where the process is itself a symbolic one—the 'commodity' that is being exchanged *is* language, or rather is a semiotic
that is realized in the form of language. It is not surprising, when
seen in this light, that the concept of information, and the ability
to exchange information, is relatively late in developing. By the age
of 9 months Nigel has a very clearly developed sense of meaning as
a mediating process: by addressing another person, and exchanging
symbols with that person, he can achieve a variety of intents—but
the act of meaning in no way constitutes the realization of those
intents. It is not until the very end of his second year that he comes
to see the exchange of meanings as a goal, as a process *sui generis*,
such that the act of meaning is itself the realization of the intent.
We have seen how this awareness of exchanging information has
evolved: it has evolved through the convergence of two lines of
development, starting from two of the elementary functions of the
protolanguage, (1) the interactional: (a) 'let's be together'; (b) shared
attention to an external object, as a form of 'togetherness'; (c) the
'naming game' ('look at this picture; now you say its name');
(d) 'what's this called?' (asking for a new name); (e) WH-questions
('fill in the gap in this account'); and (2) the personal: (a) attention
to prominence ('there's a commotion??'); (b) attention to the
environment 'that's interesting'); (c) observation, recall and prediction ('Isee/saw/will see . . .'); (d) voicing shared experience ('I'm
telling you what we both saw/heard') and (e) communicating un-
shared experience (I'm telling you what I saw/heard but you didn't').

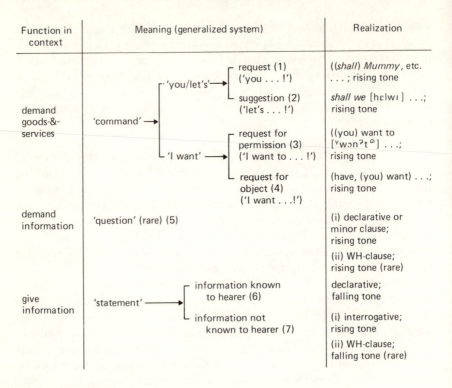

Function in context	Meaning (generalized system)	Realization

Fig. 1.14 Incipient adult (2;0): Nigel on the threshold of the adult
system of dialogue

Note: the systematic distinction between (3) and (4) is disappearing.

At the later stages there is also a third, minor strand in the process, that of 'let's explore this—what will happen?', which plays a part in the development of questions. The process can be represented in tabular form (Table 1.5). Here finally are some examples of Nigel's utterances in the period 1;11-2;0. The numbers relate to the categories in Figure 1.14.

1. Daddy carry you on shóulder
    ménd it . . . Mummy ménd it
    shall Daddy tell you the chùffa rhýme
    want Daddy to cut the séllotape
    don't wànt the peel taken óff

2. shall we go and get the toást
    shall we look at our fast dièsel train bóok

Table 1.5 The ontogeny of information

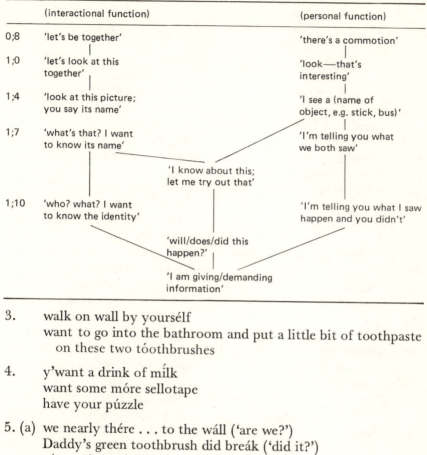

3.   walk on wall by yoursélf
     want to go into the bathroom and put a little bit of toothpaste
        on these two tóothbrushes

4.   y'want a drink of mílk
     want some móre sellotape
     have your púzzle

5. (a) we nearly thére . . . to the wáll ('are we?')
        Daddy's green toothbrush did breák ('did it?')
        gó . . . the garbage lorry gó ('does it?')
   (b) what does thát say
        how did that gone in that little hole thére

6.   the machine was making a lot of nòise
     the little bird with the long beak sitting on the wire flown
        awày
     James had a tràin
     we went in an aèroplane this morning
     Mummy put a little bit of bùtter on your arm to feel it bètter*

7. (a) did the train fall off the tráck ('the train fell . . .')

* All those in (6) are addressed to a person who had also witnessed the event; all those in
(7) are addressed to a person who had not witnessed the event.

have you eaten that toast and bútter ('I've eaten . . .')
did you get sick ('I got sick')
(b) what did Mummy dròp ('Mummy dropped something')

1.6 CONCLUSION

By the time he reaches the end of his second year, Nigel has laid the foundation for the adult system of dialogue. From here on, his meaning potential will develop along adult lines.

What was outlined in Section 1.3 was, of course, the bare bones of the system, the semantic options in their most general form. Deriving from these is the rich network of meaning potential that lies behind the conversational rhetoric of a mature speaker of the language, for whom giving and demanding information and goods-&-services is, at most, the crude raw material of conversation. The conversational process among adults displays a playful variety that, to those whose point of departure was the idealized sentence or isolated speech act of philosophical linguistics, appeared bewilderingly infinite and unstructured. To those in the ethnographic tradition, who had always worked with 'real' data, and never harboured the illusion (but did anyone?) that conversation was like the grammarian's book of rules, to go on being told this as news was simply boring. But in order to understand the system behind the conversational process it is not enough to discover 'rules of conversation'; we have to try and understand the relation of conversation to the linguistic system. The magical power of talk derives from the fact that it is, in every instance, the manifestation of a systematic resource, a resource which has been built up through acts of conversation in the first place, and which goes on being modified in each one of us as we talk our way through life.

As a final example, let us look at a very brief specimen of adult interaction; again, one that is taken from real life. A and B have met on a commuter train; they regularly do, but on this occasion they have not seen each other for some days (Passage G):

Passage G

A I see yòu're back in circulátion.
B Actually I've never been òut.
A I haven't sěen you for ages.

In this encounter, A's strategy is: 'We haven't met for some time; this is your fault, because you have failed to be where I was'. The manœuvre is so blatant that B challenges it; but he does so defen-sively, by simply denying the implication, and this allows A to return to the attack, this time with a direct accusation of I haven't seen you ('so it must be your fault'). In the first, least delicate, analysis, these are all statements; the speakers are giving information, and it is important to recognize this component in their meaning, since without it they would not work. (Note that the interpretation of these as statements is neither 'deeper' nor 'shallower' than other steps in the interpretation. It is simply less delicate, less sharply focused.) But they are also moves in a game, with its strategies of attack and defence; and this is another aspect of the social context, one that is typically realized through the semantics of praise and blame—in other words, through the values that speakers attach to acts of meaning. These values are realized in their turn by various lexicogrammatical features within the interpersonal component; such as, in this example, the adjunct of mild protest actually, and the feature 'reservation' realized by the fall-rise tone in A's second turn, meaning 'you claim you haven't been out of circulation, but I haven't seen you, so you have something to explain'.

Interpersonal meanings such as protestation and reservation are just as much part of the linguistic system as are meanings of an ideational kind. The fact that interpersonal meanings often have different modes of expression from ideational ones, being prosodic or 'field'-like in their scope rather than segmental or 'particle'-like, and hence do not lend themselves so readily to representation in a constituency framework, may be one of the reasons why they have usually been treated as unsystematic. We should suggest rather that this is a reason for rejecting constituent structure as the primary organizing concept in linguistics, and for interpreting language in functional and systemic terms. In the explanation of dialogue, whether we are concerned with the most general categories or with the subtlest distinctions, and whether the focus is on the mature system of an adult or on its ontogenesis in a child, we are concerned with meanings of the interpersonal kind; it would be a mistake to adhere rigidly to theories of language which, because they reduce all linguistic organization to one type of structure, one that is typically associated with meanings of a different kind, namely ideational ones, thereby commit themselves to treating all interpersonal meanings as something secondary or tangential.

This leads us back to questions of language as code and language as behaviour. The organization of dialogue is a systematic feature of language; it is linguistically coded behaviour. It is built up by a child as part of his total semiotic potential. Neither the system nor its evolution can be satisfactorily explained in terms of a competence-performance dichotomy in which the code is so highly idealized that it cannot be used to explain what people do. Dialogue is not 'just a matter of performance' (whatever that might mean). Nor, however, is it a matter of a special kind of competence ('communicative competence') that is somehow distinct from the ability to construct ideationally well-formed sentences. Taking part in dialogue is a dynamic process of selecting within a whole range of interrelated networks of interpersonal meanings. Interpersonal meanings are not 'uses of' ideational ones, or optional extras that sometimes get tacked on to them as an afterthought. The two constitute distinct but parallel components of the semantic system, and every act of meaning is the product of selections in both.

The significance of the semiotic perspective that is shared by the papers in this volume is that it most readily transcends the ideological gap between the philosophical and the ethnographic approaches to language. In using the term 'semiotic', we are not thinking primarily of the 'sign' in its Saussurean sense, which is not a necessary element in semiotic explanations, but rather of 'signifying'—of semiotic acts and their underlying systems. A semiotic act is any act, linguistic or otherwise, that projects cultural meanings and can be interpreted as the realization of such meanings. Acts of meaning in the linguistic sense, semantic acts, are those in which the meanings that are exchanged are coded in the form of language—the one semiotic system that evolved solely for that purpose.

NOTE

1. See sections 11.2.1-11.2.3 of Chapter 11 by Robin P. Fawcett for an introductory discussion of some of the basic concepts required in a systemic functional grammar.

BIBLIOGRAPHY

Allerton, D. J., Carney, E., and Holdcroft, D. (eds) (1979), *Function and Context in Linguistic Analysis: Essays Offered to William Haas*, Cambridge, Cambridge University Press.

Bruner, Jerome (1975), 'The ontogenesis of speech acts', *Journal of Child Language*, 2, 1-19.

Bullowa, M. (ed) (1979), *Before Speech: The Beginnings of Interpersonal Communication*, Cambridge, Cambridge University Press.

Ervin-Tripp, Susan M. (1964), 'An analysis of the interaction of language, topic and listener' in John J. Gumperz and Dell H. Hymes (eds), *The Ethnography of Communication* (*American Anthropologist*, 66.6 Part 2), 86–102.

Gumperz, J. J. and Hymes, D. H. (eds) (1964), *The Ethnography of Communication* (*American Anthropologist*, 66.6 Part 2).

Halliday, M. A. K. (1975), *Learning How to Mean: Explorations in the Development of Language*, London, Edward Arnold.

Halliday, M. A. K. (1978), *Language as Social Semiotic: the Social Interpretation of Language and Meaning*, London, Edward Arnold (also Baltimore, Md., University Park Press, 1979).

Halliday, M. A. K. (1979a), 'One child's protolanguage' in Margaret Bullowa (ed.), *Before Speech: the Beginnings of Interpersonal Communication*, Cambridge, Cambridge University Press, 171–90.

Halliday, M. A. K. (1979b), 'Modes of meaning and modes of expression: types of grammatical structure, and their determination by different semantic functions' in D. J. Allerton, Edward Carney and David Holdcroft (eds), *Function and Context in Linguistic Analysis: Essays Offered to William Haas*, Cambridge, Cambridge University Press, 57–79.

Halliday, M. A. K. and Hasan, Ruqaiya (1976), *Cohesion in English*, London, Longman (English Language Series 9).

Halliday, M. A. K. and Martin, J. R. (eds) (1981), *Readings in Systemic Linguistics*, London, Batsford Academic & Educational.

Lamb, Sydney M. (1966), 'Epilegomena to a theory of language', *Romance Philology*, 19, 531–73.

Lyons, John (1968), *Introduction to Theoretical Linguistics*, Cambridge, Cambridge University Press.

2 Metaphors of information

John Regan
Claremont Graduate School, Claremont

2.1 INTRODUCTION

Where are the sources of these data which become the information in a child's world view? What does a child know that enables him to be a member of a social situation, and what does he learn while he is learning? Specifically for this study in relation to the yet-to-be-known, where does the child visualize himself? Does he see himself at the centre of a sphere, at the end of the golden string, within a seamless web, or, as Whorf would say, on a ribbon marked off into segments waiting to be filled with an entry? Whatever this position, the viewpoint is learnt.

The data of this study are part of a three-year, cross-national project which documented comparable social settings. In the case of this paper, the situation selected is the school-room, where language is purported to be used for its heuristic function, one locus of a child's early years where he encounters the culture's epistemological metaphors.

A child is in a constant state of learning. It can therefore be presumed that no experience leaves him unaffected. But what are those experiences and of what is the commonplace composed? Artists describe it in coats of many colours. The linguist's contribution is a documentation of the communicative part of what is said, and a comparison of the result with what could be said.

Among the information learnt by the child through discourse in the school is his view of himself in the act of discovering the unknown, of knowing where to fit into the turn-taking segmentation of the discourse framework, the fine calibration of when and when not to speak, about what topics and in which contexts.

A definition of the type of information investigated in this study would be found in the answers to the following questions:

What does the child of this culture know that he knows and what does he know is available to be known?

What is the proportion of that which he knows to what he could
   know?
What are his metaphors of the nature of knowledge?
How does he believe the unknown is discovered?
How is his success in this discovery verified?

2.2 STRUCTURES OF DISCOURSE

We may go down a street every day for years without realizing that
each house is the same basic box design, that the whole is simply
two rows of identical houses built by the same contractor. The
internal similarity has been obscured by external differences. Nevertheless, all that the original blueprint included is still there. It is no
different with language. Exterior differences can so distract our
attention that the internal similarities are overlooked. By removing
external features of the discourse of classrooms we observe the
same structure. The more removed, the less the difference among
each lesson of each teacher and the more like managerial social
control discourse it is.

Sometimes we are conscious of planning what to say—the words,
the general direction of the topic. Other times we are conscious only
midway, or only after the conversation is over. But before, during
or after, we do have choices. However, within these choices, there
are rules of shared information which constitute the blueprints of
interaction. This fact is illustrated in the following examples.

My office opens on to a fairly narrow corridor in which two
people cannot pass without brushing. The result is that one person
usually steps aside. But which one? There do not seem to be any
rules, but there are. One of these concerns the number of times
we dodge—another the speed, another the angle of the sway, its
beginning and end points.

I stepped out of my door recently, set off to the right, and almost
fell directly into a colleague. There were three specific units to the
consequent verbal and nonverbal interaction. Then we both stopped,
spoke, stood sideways, and one of us went through. In the preceding
thirty or less seconds, data from all channels of communication had
operated simultaneously. Within this period the two participants
shared a knowledge of the content, span, timing, speed, angle,
duration, number of repetitions which, clustering together, constituted that brief encounter.

Participants' joint understanding manifested in such communicative units constitutes a shared backdrop in interaction such that in

each person there is a sense of such features. We sense when the first part of a conversation is over, when the second is beginning, where transitions occur.

I once observed an army friend coming back after a meeting with the colonel about a topic of career importance. When I asked how the interview had turned out he replied, 'I talked too much'. Similarly, I had seen a college roommate coming out of the office of one of his instructors with a similar despondent look. 'I said "thank you" once too often,' he muttered. Each of these individuals had gone on too long with one feature of conversation and had known that in a conscious way. These features were not physical details as in the dodging example but rather duration (in the young officer's case) and quantity (in the student's) of the verbal reply. Each is a feature about interaction known verbally or nonverbally to the participants. The interaction of every social situation—office, coffee shop, classroom—has similar unique characteristics learnt by the interactants. School children learn these in their class-rooms and while they are learning they learn something more.

While in attendance at a school acrobatic display, I observed an additional feature of these rules which has relevance to this chapter: three groups of ten children were in the performance. Each child performed a series of acrobatic turns individually across the stage while an audience of parents and peers watched. As might be expected, applause for each child varied. For example, popular children, those with large families, a child who had caught the fancy of the audience, etc., would get more applause. In addition, in the allocation of this form of praise a factor of a different sort was operating. A perform-ance by a child following immediately after heavy applause for the previous child, received—unless some idiosyncratic factor occurred —a more minor response. The next child received somewhat more, the next more. Thus, some applause seemed not simply related to performance or popularity, but also to its location in the group sequence. That had an effect on the praise, independent of the quality of tumbles. Hence a prediction of response could be made on the basis of sequence.

In studying the kilometres of classroom discourse tapes from around the classrooms across the world, one is impressed with a curious similar predictability of next steps in the teachers' dis-course. Questions and responses proceed through phases until, at points in the sequences, the answers are either drawn out by the teacher or, if given by the pupil, dependent on its placement in discourse patterns, rewarded with praise unrelated to the answers' epistemological quality. The following are examples drawn from a

corpus consisting of 36 separate classroom tapings from six countries: Australia, New Zealand, Denmark, Canada, England, and the
United States of America, principally with children in the first
2 to 3 years in government schools. Tapes from the United States
include classrooms in four ethnic communities (White, Black,
Mexican-American, Mexican-Indian); three sizes (small groups,
5 to 8 people in a group; large groups, 30 to 50, in fixed seated lessons;
and one 'open classroom'). With this material as basis we have
studied samples from 50,000 individual dyadic teacher/pupil
statements.

One teacher may so often repeat 'very good' that it functions as
no more than a head nod, whereas another's style may be such that
these words mean an impressed mark of praise. Therefore, three
degrees were identified such that after each teacher's classroom conversation was studied to establish his customary profile, that
individual's praise rating could be established. For the purpose of
this discussion, we will assume three types of praise emphasis.

(1) = 'Yes, I've heard, let's go on.'
(2) = 'I've heard and what you have said is a good answer.'
(3) = 'I've heard and what you have said is a very good answer.'

Sample I: Australia, Grade 1: (T) Teacher, (P) Pupil(s)

T   Can you think back to when I showed you a film?
P   Yes.
T   *And do you remember that in that film they kept saying that it
    was April and they were talking about spring? (*Emphasis 1)
P   Yes.
T   *And we know that it was April—here in Sydney—but it wasn't
    spring was it? (*Emphasis 1)
P   No.
T   Can you remember what it was?
P   It was autumn.
T   It was autumn. Good girl. (Emphasis 3* terminates unit and
    introduces next, which begins:)
    Now we don't do what these people are doing in these holidays
    because it's going to be too cold. It's going to be winter.
P   Winter.
T   This picture is a picture of . . . of . . . ?
P   Of boys building a sand castle.
T   *That's right . . . What time of the year is it? What's the hot time
    of the year? (*Emphasis 2).
P   Spring.
P   Summer.

T Summer. Good boy, Nicholas. (Emphasis 3 terminates unit and introduces next.)

Sample II: The United States, Grade 3

T Where is the little man now?
P Under the mushroom.
T What is he holding over his head?
P A mushroom.
T How can you tell that he is happy?
P Because he is smiling.
T *Because he's smiling! (Emphasis 2* and termination of unit.)
T All right, boys and girls, I want to read the poem. You look at the pictures and listen (reads). What was the little man called?
P A wee elf.
T A wee elf, very good. *(Emphasis 1) Was he large or small?
P Small.
T How do you know he was small?
P Because it said so in the poem.
T Because it said so in the poem. Very good. (Emphasis 2) Why did the elf want to get under the toadstool?
P Because it was raining.
T *Because it was raining. What did he do as he crept under the toadstool?
P (Guessed attempts by pupils.) (*Emphasis 1)
T He . . .
P (More guesses.)
T Or he . . .
P Trembled.
T *Trembled—all right. Why do you think he was trembling? (Emphasis 1)
P Because he was frightened—**very good Ricky.** (Emphasis 3) Why did he not want to fly away?
P Because he was afraid.
T *Right, because he was afraid. How can you know what he was thinking? (Emphasis 1)
P Because he had a happy smile.
T Because he had a happy smile. Very good. (Emphasis 2) What did he have over his head?
P A mushroom.
T Very good. (Emphasis 2)

Sample III: New Zealand, Grade 1

The Grade-1 children sitting around the teacher have learnt more than school content in the first five months at school—data upon which the foundation of their thinking about how to learn and find out may be built.

The chatter that has opened the session is a preliminary. Teacher and pupils implicitly know that. Soon this general discussion will cease and focused conversation will begin. To this point there have been numerous scattered topics: holidays, cars, grandparents, birthdays, getting ready—a predictable component in a predictable discourse sequence. The teacher's intonation gives clues that this is a prelude and that the substance of the lesson is to come. She is not completely involved, but the next phase, for 'information', is about to start. The frame marker of this is 'well then'.

T	Well then do you like this picture we've got here?
P	Yes.
P	The baby's in the kitchen.
T	*Yes. (Emphasis 1)
P	Having his tea.
T	*Yes, I wonder if it's tea, or breakfast or lunch? (Emphasis 1)
P	Tea.
T	*(Nods) (Emphasis 1)
P	I think they're doing the dishes.
T	What makes you think that?
P	Because they've got all the pots out there.
T	Yes, do you think it's at the sink that the mother's working? (Emphasis 1)
P	Yes.
T	What do you think, Kenny?
P	The sauce pans and the pans.
T	Yes. (Emphasis 1)
T	Well, what has this mother been doing? John?
Billy	She's been—
T	John?
John	Washing it.
T	Right. (Emphasis 2) And what is she doing then?
John	Putting it on the stove.
T	And what happens when you put the food on the stove, John?
John	It cooks.
T	Good boy, I like the way you thought that out. That's very good. (Emphasis praise 3 terminates unit and introduces the next.)

Sample IV: Canada, Lower Elementary Grade, Language Experience Lesson

T	What makes you think it's a country picture, Jimmy?
Mark	Because it hasn't got much houses: it's only got one.
Justin	No, two are there; I'll show you.
T	The house they're living in and . . .
Justin	I know. The other . . .
T	How do you know there's another house?
Jimmy	Because there's another house in the window.
T	Good boy. Jimmy has answered *that one beautifully.* (Emphasis 3 terminates unit and introduces· next which follows immediately.)

Sample V: England, Upper Elementary Grade, Science Lesson

T	Put your pens down; pencils down; fold your arms; look at the floor; look at the door; look at me. Good. Now. Before I came to school this morning, I had my breakfast. I had some cereal, and I had some toast, and I had an egg, and I had a cup of tea, and then I had a biscuit, and then I came to school. And you probably did the same sort of thing. I don't know what you have for breakfast: we have some weird and wonderful things. But you probably had some breakfast. And at dinnertime, in school, if you had the same dinner as me, you had fish, potatoes and cabbage, and then you had some lemon meringue and some custard, and, when you go home tonight, you'll probably have some more tea. Something else to eat. You'll fill yourself up. Perhaps with some more fish and chips. Or perhaps with just some meat and potatoes. Or perhaps with some cream cakes. And then before you go to bed, you might have something else to eat: hot drink and a sandwich and a biscuit perhaps. And then you'll climb into bed, and you'll go to sleep. Now tell me: why do you eat all that food? Can you tell me why do you eat all that food? Yes.
P	. To keep you strong.
T	To keep you strong. Yes.* To keep you strong. Why do you want to be strong? (Emphasis 1)
P	Sir,—muscles.
T	To make muscles. Yes.* Well what would you want to use —what would you want to do with your muscles? (*Emphasis 1)
P	Sir, use them.

T You'd want to—
P Use them.
T You'd want to use them.* Well how do you use your muscles?
   (*Emphasis 1)
P By working.
T By working. Yes.* And when you're working, what are you using
   apart from your muscles? What does that food give you? What
   does the food give you? (*Emphasis 1)
P Strength.
T Not only strength; we have another word for it. Yes.
P Energy.
T Good girl. Yes. Energy. You can have a team point. That's
   a very good word. (Emphasis 3, end of unit.)

2.3 DISCUSSION

There are discourse rhythms in the language of the classroom that are
as much a part of the interactant's shared awareness as are the
number of beats to corridor dodges or duration of talk. On the basis
of these also, predictions can be made:

that a new phase in the interaction is beginning;
that a termination to a unit is approaching;
that at a specific point answers to the teacher's question will be
   accepted, but not later in the unit.
that, if someone does not give it at the 'right' time, the teacher
   will give or extract the answers;
that praise 1 or 2 will be given towards the end of the unit but not
   if the answer comes at the beginning or during the first phases.

While both sides of the dyad know these rules, the child can make
'mistakes', as evidenced in the above samples. If these understandings
shared by participants of classroom interaction were applied to creating a mechanical teaching machine that asked questions and responded
according to the pupil's reply and it were to produce transcripts
such as those reported here, the program would need to include a
discourse locational factor which would act independently of the
quality of the pupil's answer. For, to be like the classroom, such
a machine would give praise to the student according to a point in
the span of discourse rather than according to the difficulty of an
answer. Such a machine program would therefore teach more than
the overt subject matter:

(1) that success is not predictable in terms of the epistemological content under discussion;
(2) that dramatic praise follows very differing achievements, some as ordinary as remembering what the teacher had just said or guessing a desired word;
(3) that information is composed of particles;
(4) that the discovery of this in the classroom proceeds from the known to the unknown, from the parts to the whole, and suggests therefore a method of dismantling knowledge, a strategy of inquiry, a metaphor of knowledge.

This would contribute to the child's view of how knowledge is acquired, his relationship to it, and provide a method of estimation that he was near to a solution. Such a machine would be operating like the talk of the teaching in the typical classroom studied.

What is precisely familiar about the classroom discourse lies in the shared understanding of:

when content begins;
the times of pupils' answers;
when their questions are allowed and disallowed;
when they are altered, extended, cut off;
when summations or transitions occur;
when praise is given; and
the intensiveness of that praise.

These, in large measure predictable events, are outward signs of an inner learning, of in fact a classroom infra language. They are a ground plan of the discourse used not for its heuristic opportunities but as a social control device. In turn, the patterns present messages about a mechanical construction of knowledge, what there is to know, where it can be discovered, its makeup, its 'beginning,' and 'end'. Information is discovered by reading approximating clues which are found, in part, in the positioning and pacing of replies. These are organizational, regulatory functioning messages which, in turn, have a deeper level of influence on the child's world view about knowledge and their relationship to it. Teacher education may reinforce these habits but the origin lies elsewhere—in mass instruction and its effects on linguistic choice. Thus, in group teaching, size and consequent organizational needs constrain the function to which interaction is used. In turn the discourse structure presents messages about a mechanical construction of knowledge, what there is to know, where it can be discovered, its structure.

Throughout the classroom samples studied there were no direct statements about the nature of knowledge and discovery. No alternative modes were implied or stated explicitly. On the other hand, there was a constant flow of implicit statements. The teacher asks the questions, knows the answers, and evaluates on the closeness to the match.

Another strand of cultural information contained in the pedagogical discourse is the nature of the public person which the child should present in particular contexts—hence the interactional skills of that public person. The child learns the characteristics of that person as far as discovery and explication of formal information and authority is concerned. He does this, in part, by learning features of the verbal interaction such as who asks what to whom, in which ways, with what results, who dispenses and receives rewards.

These roles of explicator and inquirer intermix a source of knowledge and a source of authority—a combination not equally familiar to all the social and economic groups which come together in the education institution. As Halliday has pointed out, societies which institutionalize education develop implicit methods of getting around this discrepancy of roles—the conflict between the child's conception of the semiotic function of talk and the demands that the school makes upon the functions of language at particular ages. Thus, the segmentation and structuring of classroom overt knowledge could be seen as a cultural adaptation to this discrepancy, evidence of which is found in a child's dismay that his teacher is ignorant because the teacher asked for the answer.

Formal education has complex outcomes, overt and covert aims. Among these is one related to 'inquiry', 'information', 'knowledge', 'exploration'. In the data corpus, most of the time the teacher is talking and the great majority of that talking is in the form of asking nonheuristic questions. Questions rarely come from the pupil. The question–answer response sequence repeating like a theme of a ditty—'I know; you don't; guess it if you can'—is strummed over special material and is a potential inner world-view message from which children get a particular perspective on discovery. The child's fine ear of awareness for essential features suggests that although he may not listen to the surface talk, he hears its inner form.

What is knowledge like? How is it acquired? Who knows it? These are essential questions to which children in some way find individual answers. The data presented here give skewed replies to these questions. Time-filling control requirements constrain speech to segment content in the form of turn-taking. Awareness of a tendency is one step towards evaluating the implications of that disposition. Educators in mass institutions could be provided with explicit information on the patterns identified.

Other directions of study, including that contained in the pedagogical linguistic system messages, could be explored. For example, the child's name is used only in relation to praise or blame, either of behaviour and/or giving information. In addition, there is the lexical association of 'good/bad' with personal name. In early home experiences the child experiences these terms in relation to others' evaluation of their behaviour rather than in connection with knowledge and discovery. The same lexical items of praise/blame are used also for marking epistemological as well as authority/social structure pupil responses.

Language and culture can be viewed as two possibly intertwined semiotic systems and spoken interaction as both a reflection of the social structure and specifically a presentation of self in learning/explaining situations. This chapter has presented data on some of the cultural information discoverable in language in its function as a transmitter of culture. It is a record of a language—an infra language all have heard but have not recognized, composed of levels of choices principally made unconsciously. The implications of those choices in the undercurrent of school dialogue present deafening messages to the mind contained in the seeming silence of unnoticed comments. Indeed, many presently puzzling questions about human development will be found to have a close connection with the patterns of this infra-language, a description of which is a prerequisite for any generation of hypotheses about the socialization power of discourse in home or school.

The observations reported describe one locus of socialization, the mass urban classroom, as an example of the constraints of context on implicit linguistic alternatives choice. It is an illustration first of a relation between the deeper theoretical interest of the symposium theme and of educational research originating from the broader basis of anthropological linguistics.

3 How universal is a localist hypothesis? A linguistic contribution to the study of 'semantic styles' of language

Yoshihiko Ikegami
University of Tokyo, Japan

3.1 THE LOCALIST THESIS IN THE HISTORY OF LINGUISTICS

In the history of linguistics, the localists are known as those people who contended that the meaning of the grammatical case could be accounted for in terms of a set of notions which refer to spatial relationships. Their basic tenet was given by Wüllner, one of the leading exponents of the localist theory, as follows:

> Alles Denken und Sprechen geht von Anschauung aus und zieht darauf zurück. Alle Anschauung aber ist an Raum und Zeit geknüpft, und die Anschauung dieser beiden und ihre möglichen Beziehungen sind gleichsam die Formen für alles Anschauen. [Wüllner 1827:8]

Similarly, in the words of another representative localist, Hartung:

> Unsere Wahrnehmung geschieht theils durch die Sinne theils durch den Geist. Die sinnliche Wahrnehmung geht überall voran: dieser dient darum auch die Sprache früher als der geistigen. Vermöge der Analogie des Geistigen und Sinnlichen wird dann das Wort auf die geistige Wahrnehmung übertragen. [Hartung 1831:4]

The localists believed and tried to demonstrate that underlying all the apparently diversified uses of the cases are such 'concrete' spatial notions as 'movement from', 'movement to', and 'location at' and that the former are no more than transfers from or manifestations of the latter at less concrete levels.[1]

3.2 A VERB-CENTRED REFORMULATION OF THE THESIS

In this paper, we are not going to discuss directly the merits and demerits of the traditional localists. Rather we will be concerned with exploring the explanatory potentials of their thesis as applied to a somewhat different area. Instead of concerning ourselves, like the localists, with the meaning of the case—the case being understood by them almost always as a surface category—we will consider the semantic structure underlying the linguistic representation of 'change' and 'state'. That is, we will ask whether there exists a set of basic patterns underlying the various linguistic expressions referring to an event called 'change' or 'state' and whether such basic patterns can be identified with those which serve to represent the most concrete types of 'change' and 'state', namely, 'change in locus' and 'existence in locus'. By making an inquiry along such lines, we will obviously be placing ourselves in a far wider perspective than the traditional localists. Since an extralinguistic event which may linguistically be represented can be either a 'change' or a 'state', it follows that if we define a set of semantic patterns employed by language in representing the 'change'-type and the 'state'-type of events, we will then be in possession of a complete scheme of structural patterns which language employs in representing an infinite variety of events in the outer world.

3.3 SURFACE CUES TO COMMON UNDERLYING PATTERNS

Cues for positing a set of common underlying patterns will easily be found if we review sentences like the following.[2]

3.3.1 First, there are obvious examples like the following in which the common underlying patterns are more or less reflected in the surface construction:

1. Two people are in the room. (Existence)
2. Two people are in the wrong. (Condition)
3. John has a watch. (Possession).
4. John has a cold. (Condition)
5. The ball went to John. (Change in locus)
6. First prize went to John. (Change in possessorship)
7. John came to the station. (Change in locus)
8. John came to life. (Change in condition).
9. A beggar came to the archbishop. (Change in locus)
10. Death came to the archbishop. (Change in condition)
11. John got money. (Change in possessorship)
12. John got fame. (Change in condition)

3.3.2 Second, there are pairs of 'cognitively synonymous' sentences 'transformationally' related to each other:

13. There are two windows in the room. (Existence)
14. The room has two windows. (Existence)
15. Two of these books belong to Mary. (Possession)
16. Mary has two of these books. (Possession)
17. A letter came to me. (Change in locus)
18. I received a letter. (Change in locus)
19. First prize went to Mary. (Change in possessorship)
20. Mary got first prize. (Change in possessorship)

3.3.3 In terms of individual words, we often notice cases of polysemy with regard to the different types of change or state. See the uses of the verbs be, have, go, come and get as illustrated in 3.3.1. Have and get are further used as causative verbs for any time of change (as in have him come and get him to come). Get is also a change-in-locus verb in such a use as get to the station. Also to be noted are such verbs as send representing a change in locus (send a person to the hospital) and a change in condition (send a person to death) and give representing a change in possessorship (give a present to a person) and a change in condition (give a person to understand). Further consider the use of German geben and French avoir to represent spatial existence (as in es gibt and il y a) or of English obtain to represent existence or condition (as in this custom no longer obtains).

3.3.4 There are examples of a pair of cognate words, one of which refers to one notion while the other to another. Cp. English become as a change-in-condition verb and German bekommen as a change-in-possessorship verb. There is also an obvious etymological relation between English come as a change-in-locus verb and become as a change-in-condition verb.

3.3.5 There are also cases in which one and the same grammatical function is fulfilled by a verb referring to one of the three notions in one language while another language represents the same function by a verb referring to another of the same three notions. Thus in representing the action passive, English often uses the typically change-in-possessorship verb get, while German has the typically change-in-condition verb werden. It may be recalled that in Old English the auxiliary for the passive was weorþan ('to become'), cognate of German werden.

3.3.6 After reviewing these examples, it will not be difficult to suppose that some common structural patterns underlie the pairs of superficially different sentences such as the following:

21. John went to the station.
22. John went crazy. (i.e. 'John went to "the state of being crazy" ')
23. John was in the room.
24. John was wrong. (i.e. 'John was in "the state of being wrong" ')
25. John got fame.
26. John got famous. (i.e. 'John got "the state of being famous" ' or 'John got to "the state of being famous" ')
27. She sent John to the hospital.
28. She sent John crazy. (i.e. 'She sent John to "the state of being crazy" ', 'She caused John to go to "the state of being crazy" ')
29. John kept his hands in his pockets.
30. John kept his arms straight. (i.e. 'John kept his arms in "the state of being straight" ', 'John caused his arm to remain in "the state of being straight" ')
31. He gave his daughter to John.
32. He gave his daughter to understand that she had to marry John. (i.e. 'He caused his daughter to go to "the state of understanding . . ." ')

With a little more stretch of imagination, it will not be difficult to suppose that the same structural patterns may underlie expressions like the following:

33. John became crazy. (i.e., 'John came to the "the state of being crazy" ')
34. John became a doctor. (i.e. 'John came to "the state of being a doctor" ')
35. John was a doctor. (i.e. 'John was in "the state of being a doctor" ')
36. It made John crazy. (i.e. 'It caused John to go to "the state of being crazy" ')
37. It made John cry. (i.e. 'It caused John to go to "the state of crying" ')
38. Father made John a doctor. (i.e. 'Father caused John to go to "the state of being a doctor" ')
39. Father kept John busy. (i.e. 'Father caused John to remain in "the state of being busy" ')

3.4 FORMALIZATION OF UNDERLYING STRUCTURAL PATTERNS

The common structural patterns underlying these and other related sentences can be shown in a formalized way as follows.[3]

3.4.1 There are three fundamental categories to be taken note of: namely, (a) something which moves, (b) the goal, and (c) the movement undergone, for 'change', and (a) something which exists, (b) the location, and (c) the state of existence, for 'state', Representing (a) as X and (b) as Y, and (c) as $\rightarrow$ (for 'change') and $>$ (for 'state'), respectively, we will represent a 'change' and a 'state' in their most fundamental forms as follows:

$X \rightarrow Y$ (i.e. X GO/COME TO Y or X BECOME WITH Y)
$X > Y$ (i.e. X BE WITH Y).

3.4.2 One of the two terms, either X or Y, is selected as 'theme'— the theme here being understood as performing a function of bringing the term in question to the sentence-initial position.[4] This gives the following possibilities:

	CHANGE	STATE
X=theme	$X \rightarrow Y$	$X > Y$
Y=theme	$Y \leftarrow X$	$Y < X$

The contrast is seen, for example, between sentences (13) and (14), (15) and (16), (17) and (18), and (19) and (20) in 3.3.2.

3.4.3 Either of the two terms, X and Y, can be either 'concrete' or 'abstract'. If both X and Y are concrete and the change is also concrete (i.e. physically measurable), then we have a change in locus. Thus,

X=theme   A letter (Conc.) came to John (Conc.)
Y=theme   John (Conc.) received a letter (Conc.).

If both X and Y are concrete and the change is abstract (i.e. not physically measurable), then we have a change in possessorship. Thus,

X=theme   The farm (Conc.) went to John (Conc.).
Y=theme   John (Conc.) got the farm (Conc.).

If either or both of X and Y is/are abstract (in which case the change is necessarily abstract), then we have a change in condition. Thus,

X=theme	Victory (Abst.) went to the visiting team (Conc.).
Y=theme	The visiting team (Conc.) got victory (Abst.).
X=theme	John (Conc.) fell into a bad habit (Abst.).
Y=theme	A bad habit (Abst.) got John (Conc.).
X=theme	A sudden end (Abst.) came to their happy life (Abst.).
Y=theme	Their happy life (Abst.) came to a sudden end (Abst.).

Since a 'state' can be conceived of as resulting from a 'change', one can reasonably expect that the same argument applies to the state as well. We thus have the following classification:

X	Y	→/>	CHANGE	STATE
concrete	concrete	concrete	— Change in locus	Spatial existence
concrete	concrete	abstract	— Change in possessorship	Possession
concrete	abstract	abstract ⎤		
abstract	concrete	abstract ⎥ —	Change in condition	Condition
abstract	abstract	abstract ⎦		

3.4.4 When the structural formulas as given in 4.2 are linguistically represented, there are some complications involved. We will discuss this point mainly with regard to the representation of 'change', assuming that a parallel argument can be made about the representation of 'state'.

The representation of the X=theme formula is fairly straightforward. Ideally, we have X and Y, a verb of motion (concrete or abstract), and a goal marker. We will represent this as X GO/COME TO Y.[5]

The representation of the Y=theme formula involves two possibilities. In one case, Y (with its goal marker deleted) is preposed with a concomitant structural change; in the other case, Y (with its goal marker) is preposed with essentially no further structural change. We will represent the two possibilities as Y RECEIVE X and TO Y GO/COME X for the change in locus and Y GET X and TO Y GO/COME X for the change in possessorship and the change in condition.

For the restructured Y=theme pattern, there is a possibility of ambiguity as to the direction of motion whenever the motion is abstract. Thus a change-in-possessorship sentence like **John got the**

farm, which realizes the pattern Y GET X, can be interpreted not only as 'John had the farm come to him' $(Y \leftarrow X)$ but also as 'John went to (the state of possessing) the farm' or 'John got to (the state of possessing) the farm' $(Y \rightarrow X)$. Similarly, a change-in-condition sentence like **John got/became old** can be interpreted either as 'John had oldness come to him' $(Y \leftarrow X)$ or as 'John got/came to oldness' $(Y \rightarrow X)$. We will represent the second interpretation as Y BECOME WITH X. Thus there are two possible restructured Y=theme patterns for the change in possessorship and the change in condition, namely, Y GET X and Y BECOME WITH X. The same ambiguity does not seem to arise in the case of change in locus, where the motion is concrete and hence its direction is perceptually identifiable.

3.4.5 We have then the following scheme of structural patterns as linguistic representation of the three types of change:

Change in Locus

X=theme	X GO/COME TO Y		
Y=theme	Y RECEIVE X		TO Y GO/COME X

Change in Possessorship

X=theme	X GO/COME TO Y		
Y=theme	Y GET X	Y BECOME WITH X	TO Y GO/COME X

Change in Condition

X=theme	X GO/COME TO Y		
Y=theme	Y GET X	Y BECOME WITH X	TO Y GO/COME X

Without going into a detailed discussion, we give below the scheme of structural patterns for the three types of state. The correspondence with the scheme for the three types of change given above will be obvious.

Spatial Existence

X=theme	X BE WITH Y		
Y=theme	Y HAVE X		WITH Y BE X

Possession

X=theme	X BE WITH Y		
Y=theme[6]	Y HAVE X	Y BE WITH X	WITH Y BE X

Condition

 X=theme X BE WITH Y

 Y=theme Y HAVE X Y BE WITH X WITH Y BE X

3.4.6 We next discuss the structural patterns involving the causative.[7] In terms of the localist hypothesis, such patterns can be interpreted as deriving from a formula involving three terms: X (something which moves), Y (the goal) and Z (the source, namely, the point from which the motion starts): X GO/COME FROM Z TO Y. From this formula, two types of causative are derived. In one case, the source happens to be animate and this animate source is thematized and reinterpreted as 'agent'; in the other case, the goal happens to be animate and this animate goal is thematized and reinterpreted as 'experiencer'.[8] We will represent the two types of causative as follows:

 W (agent: deriving from animate source) CAUSE [S]
 W (experiencer: deriving from animate goal) GET–HAVE [S]

where S represents any of the (non-causative) structural patterns given in 3.4.2.

The causative formula can linguistically be represented in two ways, depending on whether 'incorporation' is involved or not.[9] Incorporation seems to be incomparably more common for the 'agent'-type of causative than for the 'experiencer'-type of causative. Below is given a scheme of structural patterns for the 'agent'-type of incorporated causative for 'change':

Change in Locus

 X=theme   SEND X TO Y

 Y=theme   SEND Y X SEND TO Y X

Change in Possessorship

 X=theme   GIVE X TO Y

 Y=theme[10] GIVE Y X PROVIDE Y WITH X GIVE TO Y X

Change in Condition

 X=theme   DO X TO Y

 Y=theme   DO Y X MAKE Y WITH X DO TO Y X

3.5 CONTRASTIVE REALIZATION IN ENGLISH AND JAPANESE

We have defined a general scheme for linguistically representing a change and a state. Individual languages may differ as to which patterns they choose to realize as surface forms and which patterns they leave unexploited.[11] In the following, a comparison is made between English and Japanese against the framework we have set up.

3.5.1

(i) Change in Locus

English

X=theme	X GO/COME TO Y
Y=theme	Y RECEIVE X

Japanese[12]

X=theme	X ga Y e/ni YUKU/KURU	
Y=theme	(Y ga X o UKETORU)	Y e/ni X ga YUKU/KURU

Both in English and Japanese, the X=theme pattern is more commonly employed than the Y=theme pattern. In Japanese, the Y=theme pattern is realized commonly by a simple permutation of the two terms. In English, this will be possible only if Y is decidedly a marked theme (e.g. **To John came a letter**); hence not cited above. The realization of the restructured Y=theme pattern is considerably restricted in either language. Thus in English, **A letter came to John** and **John received a letter** constitute a pair, but not **John came to the station** and ***The station received John**. Moreover, the Japanese verb UKETORU is a compound (UKE = 'receive', TORU = 'take'); hence the realizational possibility is shown in parentheses.

(ii) Change in Possessorship

English

X=theme	X GO/COME TO Y
Y=theme	Y GET X

Japanese

X=theme	
Y=theme	Y ga X o MORAU

Unlike the change-in-locus expressions, the Y=theme pattern is more commonly employed here than the X=theme pattern. This is especially the case with Japanese, where an English sentence like **First prize went to John** can only be clumsily rendered as a sort of change-in-condition expression (approximately, 'became the possession of John'). Cp. also 3.8.1.

(iii) Change in Condition

English

X=theme	X GO/COME TO Y	
Y=theme	Y GET X	Y BECOME X

Japanese

X=theme	
Y=theme	Y ga X ni NARU

The situation is similar to that for the change in possessorship. The Y=theme pattern is the rule in Japanese. In English, the contiguity marker WITH in the pattern, Y BECOME WITH X, is realized as zero and the contrast between this pattern and the pattern, Y GET X, is virtually neutralized. (Cp. 3.4.3.)

3.5.2

(i) Change in Locus (causative)

English

X=theme	SEND X TO Y
Y=theme	SEND Y X

Japanese

X=theme	X o Y e/ni OKURU
Y=theme	Y e/ni X o OKURU

The realizations in English and Japanese closely parallel each other here.

(ii) Change in Possessorship (causative)

English

X=theme	GIVE X TO Y	
Y=theme	GIVE Y X	PROVIDE Y WITH X

Japanese

X=theme	X o Y ni AGERU/KURERU
Y=theme	Y ni X o AGERU/KURERU

Japanese has a contrast between '*Y*=1st person' and '*Y*=non-1st person'—a contrast which is characteristically seen between the change-in-locus verbs, KURU and YUKU. Of the two *Y*=theme patterns possible to English, Japanese has no counterpart to the pattern, PROVIDE *Y* WITH *X*.

(iii) Change in Condition (causative)

English

X=theme	DO *X* TO *Y*	
Y=theme	DO *Y X*	MAKE *YX*

Japanese

X=theme	*X* o *Y* ni SURU	
Y=theme	*Y* ni *X* o SURU	*Y* o *X* ni SURU

The realizations in the two languages are superficially parallel to each other, but there is an interesting difference. Japanese has a contrast between the two *Y*=theme patterns as to the kind of abstracts that can stand for *X*. Thus the pattern, *Y* ni *X* o SURU, admits of such abstracts as 'explanation', 'greeting', 'promise', 'shaking hands', 'talk', 'trick', etc., while the pattern, *Y* o *X* ni SURU, allows of such abstracts as 'elegance', 'happiness', 'illness', 'poverty', 'safety', etc. The result is a linguistic classification of abstracts into 'activity' and 'state'. It is tempting to speculate that the same distinction may have underlain the contrast between the two *Y*=theme patterns for English, namely, DO *Y X* and MAKE *Y X*; in Modern English, at any rate, the contrast is largely neutralized.[13] Notice that the realization of WITH as zero for MAKE *Y* (WITH) *X* parallels the zero realization of WITH in *X* BECOME (WITH) *X*.

3.5.3

(i) Spatial existence

English

X=theme	*X* BE WITH *Y*
Y=theme	*Y* HAVE *X*

Japanese

X=theme	*X* ga *Y* ni ARU/IRU	
Y=theme		*Y* ni *X* ga ARU/IRU

For the *Y*=theme pattern, English has a special verb HAVE, while Japanese simply permutes *X* and *Y*, using the BE-type of verb as for the X=theme pattern. The choice between ARU and IRU in Japanese depends in general on whether X is inanimate or animate.

(ii) Possession

English

| X=theme | X BELONG TO Y |
| Y=theme | Y HAVE X |

Japanese

| X=theme | X ga Y ni ARU/IRU |
| Y=theme | (Y ga X o MOTTE-IRU) | Y ni X ga ARU/IRU |

Both in English and Japanese, the Y=theme pattern is by far the commoner. The realization in Japanese, however, is essentially a transfer of the patterns for spatial existence. The Japanese direct counterpart of the English HAVE is a compound (i.e. MOT-TE 'holding', IRU 'be'); hence the pattern is given in parentheses.

(iii) Condition

English

| X=theme | X BE WITH Y |
| Y=theme | Y HAVE X | Y BE (WITH) X |

Japanese

| X=theme | X ga Y ni ARU |
| Y=theme | Y ga X de ARU | / te IRU / $\emptyset$ | Y ni X ga ARU |

The X=theme pattern, with something abstract as theme, is by far the less common both in English and Japanese. For the Y=theme pattern, English has a choice between HAVE and BE; in the latter case, the contiguity marker WITH is realized as zero whenever X is represented in the surface structure as a predicate adjective or noun. The two Y=theme patterns in Japanese represent Y BE WITH X and WITH Y BE X. The choice among de-ARU, te-IRU and $\emptyset$ for the former depends on whether X is represented as a noun (referring to a 'condition') or a verbal participle (referring to an 'activity') or an adjective.

3.6 FOCUS ON vs. SUPPRESSION OF AGENTIVITY

If we review the realizations we have described for English and Japanese, we will notice a contrast between the two languages in at least the following two points: (1) the transfer of the verbs of motion (i.e. the change-in-locus expressions) to the other spheres, and (2) the realization of the *Y*=theme pattern. To these is to be added a third point, namely, (3) the use of the 'agent'-type and the 'experiencer'-type of causative. In the following, we will discuss the three points and try to see if the contrast in these respects can be interpreted as manifesting some more general underlying principles.

Firstly, English and Japanese show a marked contrast as to the extent to which the expressions of change in locus are transferred to the other less concrete types of change. In English, GO and COME can be used in the *X*=theme expressions not only to represent a change in locus but also a change in possessorship and a change in condition: e.g. **First prize went to John, The house went to ruin, John went crazy.** In Japanese, however, a word-for-word translation of the English expressions just given is not possible; if they have to be rendered at all, they must be rendered by the verb for change in condition, NARU 'to become'. In English, the transfer goes to such an extent that an instance of spatial existence or condition is represented by a verb of motion. Sentences like the following, quoted by Hockett (1954: 117) and commented on as impossible in Chinese, are not natural for Japanese, either:

40. The land falls ten feet behind the house.
41. The road runs around the lake.

The organization of the language on the basis of spatial relationships may go further and even certain syntactico-semantic categories can be shown as fitting the localistic patterns.[14] Thus, if we represent the source, the goal and the (neutral) location as FROM *Y* / TO *Y*,[15] TO *Y* and WITH *Y*, respectively, major adverbial categories can be arranged as follows:

FROM *Y*/ TO *Y̅*		TO *Y*	WITH *Y*
TIME		TIME	TIME
(SINCE)		(TILL)	(WHILE, WHEN)
REASON	PURPOSE	RESULT	
	SUPPOSITION		
	CONCESSION		
	(SUPPOSITION		
	+BUT)		
			MEANS
			ATTENDANT
			CIRCUMSTANCES

For example, sentences like the following can be represented, in terms of their semantic structure, as shown below:

42. John has been sleeping since I left.
42'. S (=John has been sleeping) + FROM Y (=I left)
43. John had been sleeping until I came.
43'. S (=John had been sleeping) + TO Y (=I came)
44. John was sleeping while I was away [when I called].
44'. S (=John was sleeping) + WITH Y (=I was away [I called])
45. Mary was disappointed because of John's failure [because John failed].
45'. S (=Mary was disappointed) + FROM Y (=John failed)
46. John worked hard for success [in order that he might succeed].
46'. S (=John worked hard) + TO $\overline{Y}$ (=John would succeed)
47. To Mary's disappointment, John failed. [John failed, with the result that Mary was disappointed.]
47'. S (=John failed) + TO Y (=Mary was disappointed)
48. If you hear him speak [To hear him speak], you will think he is a native speaker.
48'. TO $\overline{Y}$ (=You hear him speak) + S (=you will think . . .)

Furthermore, an arrangement like the following seems to be possible for certain grammatical categories:

FROM Y / TO $\overline{Y}$	TO Y	WITH Y
PROSPECTIVE (BE TO)	PERFECTIVE (HAVE-EN)	DURATIVE (BE-ING)
INFINITIVE	PAST PARTICIPLE	PRESENT PARTICIPLE

For example, compare **a bride to be, a drowned man** and **a drowning man.**

If we introduce into our scheme the 'negative' location (WITH $\overline{Y}$: i.e. 'in some place other than Y') in parallel to the 'negative' goal (TO Y), then we can make the following arrangement for the tense and the mood:

WITH Y	WITH $\overline{Y}$ / WITHOUT Y
PRESENT	PAST
	FUTURE
INDICATIVE	SUBJUNCTIVE

Although the tense and mood categories can thus be conceived of as fundamentally deictic categories based on the contrast between

'HERE' and 'THERE' (exceptions are such mood categories as imperative and optative—which we will not discuss here), they can also be redistributed along the directional axis as follows:

FROM Y / TO $\overline{Y}$ TO Y WITH Y

FUTURE   PAST   PRESENT

The correspondence with the aspect categories discussed above may be noted and one can speculate on the alleged shift from the aspectual to the tense categories in Indo-European.

There is one very interesting implication that we can derive from the scheme above, namely, that the categories representing the source (FROM Y) are in general less established than those representing the goal (TO Y). Thus compare the prospective with the perfective aspect, the future with the past tense, and the future participle (whose function is taken over by the infinitive in English) with the past participle. This can be interpreted as a manifestation of the general tendency in which the source is much more optional than the goal (cp. **He ran to the station** and **?He ran from the station**). One can also consider in this respect the frequency with which the causer (which can be identified as originally an animate source: cp. 3.4.4) is linguistically not realized: e.g. **The door was opened** or **The door opened** instead of **The door was opened by John**.

Anything which comes close to a neat classification like this is extremely hard to conceive of for Japanese, where a number of particles and auxiliaries are employed to represent delicately divergent temporal–modal–aspectual meanings.

If 'change in locus' can be said to be a fairly dominant theme in the organization of the English language, what is then the corresponding theme for Japanese? The Japanese counterpart, so far as is shown by our linguistic data, will perhaps be the notion of '(change in) condition'. We have already referred to the fact that the English verbs of motion in their transferred uses as verbs representing a change in possessorship or in condition must be translated by a change-in-condition verb in Japanese. There is also a sense in which the Japanese counterparts of English verbs like **run, walk, swim, fly, creep, ride, drive**, etc. are not really verbs of motion in a strict sense of the word. Thus while with the English verbs one can quite naturally say, **run to the station, swim to the shore, ride to the wood**, etc., the corresponding Japanese expressions must involve either the verb IKU ('go') or KURU ('come') and be phrased as something like 'go running to the station', 'go swimming to the shore', 'go riding to the wood', etc. Without the support of IKU ('go') or KURU ('come'), the expressions would have to be made something like 'run till [up to] the station', 'swim till [up to] the shore', etc., where 'running', 'swimming', etc. are represented as a process (or almost as a state) which continues up to a certain moment rather than as a motion directed to a certain goal.[16]

3.6.1 On the basis of the preceding discussion, it appears as if the contrast between English and Japanese can broadly be characterized as one between focus on 'change in locus' and '(change in) condition'. We now want to consider what such a contrast implies in general.

One important point is that in the expressions for the change in possessorship and in condition, the possibility of interpreting the term X explicitly as agent tends to be suppressed, because in these types of change the focus is laid on the result, rather than the process itself, of the change. Thus in a sentence like **John got the farm**, **John got famous** or **John became a millionaire**, it would seem somewhat irrelevant to inquire whether John is to be interpreted as an agent or not. The tendency is naturally more marked in the case of the expression of a state, since the term X is there represented as stationary and whatever possibility there is of its functioning as agent must necessarily remain only potential. In short, the contrast between 'change in locus' and '(change in) condition' is closely correlated with the contrast between 'emphasis on agentivity' and 'suppression of agentivity'.

This brings us to our second point in which English and Japanese are in marked contrast. By reviewing the realizations we have described for the two languages, we will see that English tends to prefer the restructured type of Y=theme expression (with a different verb from the one used in the X=theme expression), while Japanese tends to get along with one and the same verb for both patterns, the different thematization being represented by simply permuting the two terms, X and Y. What this difference implies will most characteristically be seen with regard to the realization of the patterns for change in possessorship and for possession. The normal pattern for representing a change in locus or spatial existence is with X (something which moves or something which exists) rather than with Y (the goal or the location) as theme; compare the relative instability of the corresponding Y=theme pattern, on the use of which rather heavy restrictions are usually placed (cp. 3.5.1). There is, however, one situation in which Y rather than X may claim more of our attention—namely, one in which Y is animate. Since the notion of possession is only possible with an animate being, the Y=theme pattern seems to be universally the more favoured one here. The emphasis on potential agentivity, however, can be manifested in two ways: either by the simple permutation of the two terms, X and Y—in which case the term Y is still marked as goal or location—or by providing a new verb for its predicate—in which case Y has its goal or location marker deleted and is reinstalled as subject. Of the two possibilities, it is the latter in which the animacy (and hence potential agentivity) is more highlighted. The contrast in this respect is not very remarkable in the case of the expressions of change in possessorship, where a new verb is provided both in English and Japanese. In the expressions of possession, however, Japanese has a marked predilection for the former type of choice, while English decidedly opts for the latter type. The notion of animacy, which is presupposed by that of agentivity, is more highlighted in English than in Japanese.[17]

The same contrast is manifested in yet another point, namely, the realization of the causative patterns, which is our third point. English and Japanese differ markedly from each other in the extent to which the use is made of the 'experiencer'-type of causative. Thus suppose there is an event in which John did something and it affected Mary (either favourably or unfavourably). Linguistically, this event can be described in two ways: (a) with John (i.e. the person whose act affected someone else) as theme and (b) with Mary (i.e. the person who is affected by someone else's act) as theme. English will offer expressions like the following: (a) **John did it for [against] Mary,**[18] (b) **Mary got John to [Mary had John] do it (for her), Mary got [had] it done by John.** Two things can be pointed out about the realization in English: first, pattern (a) is perhaps more commonly employed than pattern (b), and second, the (b)-type of expression can be ambiguous; thus instead of being understood as one who was affected, Mary can also be interpreted as one who caused John to do it.[19] The preference for the (a)-type expression with agent as theme, coupled with the tendency to impose an agentive interpretation even on the (b)-type expression where originally an affected person rather than the causer is involved, clearly points to the strong tendency of focusing on agentivity in English. In Japanese, on the other hand, the (b)-type expression is as common as the (a)-type expression, the former represented by the use of the quasi-auxiliary MORAU ('get') or the auxiliary of the so-called 'passive' -RERU and the latter by the quasi-auxiliary AGERU/KURERU ('give') (cp. 3.5.2). Besides, there exists in Japanese no ambiguity such as the one which characterizes the English (b)-type expression. Here again the two languages differ as to the emphasis they lay on the notion of agentivity.

3.6.2 In a language with marked emphasis on agentivity, the characteristic way of representing an event will naturally be AGENT + ACT. On the other hand, in a language with a tendency towards suppression of agentivity, the agent is viewed as no more than one of the elements which participate in the event, so that the notion of the (all-inclusive) EVENT comes out paramount and that of the agent is, as it were, more or less submerged in it. If we compare the three types of change as to the contrast between 'AGENT + ACT' and 'EVENT', we will immediately notice that the former is most characteristic of the change in locus and the latter of the less concrete types of change, namely, change in possessorship and change in condition (the latter in particular). Further, if we contrast 'change' in general with 'state' in general, it is unquestionably the latter which is more clearly characterized with suppressed agentivity. Something which remains stationary is less conspicuous to the human perception than something which is undergoing a change; it fails to assert itself and hence gets more easily submerged in the totality of situation.

It will be instructive to consider in this connection one feature of the Japanese honorific language. It is in general the case that in the honorific language, direct reference to the person to be respected is avoided as much as possible. In other words, the notion of agentivity as regards such a person must be suppressed. One means of achieving this effect is to represent the person in question with a locative rather than an agent marker. Yet another way of doing this is to represent an act referring to the person to be respected as if it were a change in condition. Thus where the non-honorific language says (the Japanese equivalent of) 'He ran', the honorific language would prefer saying something like 'In him, became to-run', i.e. 'In him, came to pass (an act of) running'.[20] By moulding the whole expression into that of change in condition and by representing the actor as a location in which an event takes place, the effect of suppressing the agentivity is obtained.

Thus the contrast between English and Japanese, as seen with regard to the way in which these languages organize the extra-linguistic events, may be characterized at a very general level as one between the 'AGENT + ACT' type vs. the 'EVENT' type. To illustrate the difference in orientation by a simple example, the former is a type of language which says, 'Spring comes' and the latter is of a type which says '(It) springs'.

A parallel situation holds for the causative expressions. Thus while one type of language would say, 'John was killed in the accident', suggesting the working of an unspecified causer, the other type of languge would tend to say, 'John died in the accident', with no implication of a causer. One way of characterizing the two types would be 'DO-language' and 'BECOME-language'.

3.7 TESTIMONIES REFERRING TO THE SAME TYPE OF CONTRAST

The idea that there are two such contrasting types of language seems to be not entirely new. Thus compare the following statements:

Finck (1909: '. . . lassen sich die in der Wirklichkeit verlaufenden Vorgänge zu zwei Grüppen vereinigen: es findet entweder eine Bewegung statt, die sich meist als eine von uns ausgehende Handlung oder *Tat* darstellt, oder eine von aussen an uns herantretende, aus *Empfindungen* bestehende Wahrnehmung.' (14; cp. also 35)

Weisgerber (1963): '. . . Sehweise, bei der ein Geschehen also vorwiegend von einem Täter abhängig (in Gang gebracht) erscheint, und Sehweise, die gewissermassen täterfern bleibt und die Aufmerksamkeit stärker bei dem Geschehen selbst (Verbgefüge) und dessen Erscheinungsort verweilen lässt . . . .' (48)

Whorf (1956): 'The Indo-European languages . . . give great prominence to a type of sentence having two parts . . .—substantives and verbs—. . . . Since then, the contrast has been stated in logic in many different ways: subject and predicate, actor and action . . . the notion became so ingrained that one of these classes of entities can exist without an entity of the other class, the 'thing' class, as a peg to hang on.' (241)

Herrfahrdt (1938): 'Den entscheidenden Unterschied im Wesen der Japanischen und des Indogermanischen möchte ich in den Satz fassen: das Japanische ist eine naturgewachsene Erlebnissprache, das Indogermanische eine logisch geformte Aussagesprache.' (165)[21]

Sakuma (1941): 'I think there is a fundamental difference in attitude between the European and the Japanese expression. If the European mode of expression in this respect (i.e. the preference of the personal to the impersonal expression) can be characterized as 'human-orientated', then the Japanese type of expression may be termed 'nature-orientated' or 'de-humanized'.' (211)

'While Japanese has a tendency to represent things as "becoming so and so", a language like English seems to tend to say "somebody does so" or "be caused by somebody to do so".' (214, my translation)

P. Hartmann (1952): '. . . während ein indogermanischer Verbalaus-
druck keine Feststellung wiedergeben kann, ohne ihren Akt als
solchen so mit einem Subjekt zu verbinden, dass er garnicht ohne
diesen Bezug gedacht werden kann, werden im Japanischen die
Vorgänge "an sich" gesehen und dargestellt:' (71)

'(Im Japanischen) der Mensch wird so in dem für sein Leben
entscheidenden Kontakt mit der Umwelt nicht als ein selbst-
ständiges Wesen gesehen, das von sich aus von der Welt Besitz
ergreift, sondern als ein von Vorgängen "affiziertes Objekt".
. . . die Dinge, an denen sie (Vorgänge) sich abspielen, werden
als Orte im weitesten Sinne gesehen: dem indogermanischen
bewirkenden Tätersubjekt eintspricht im Japanischen ein Bereich,
in den ein Vorgang gehört;' (115)

Martinet (1958): 'L'action y est présenté en elle-même, SANS
ORIENTATION PAR RAPPORT AUX PARTICIPANTS, comme
elle peut l'être dans un substantif.' (386: referring to the Basque
language)

H. Hartmann (1954): 'Das menschliche Ich, das sich nach indogermanischer Konzeption als "Subjekt" und Ausgangspunkt
des Handels fühlt, tritt zurück und ordnet sich in einen Kraft-
vorgang ein.' (33: referring to the Irish language)

Whorf (1956): 'The Hopi microcosm seems to have analyzed reality
in terms of EVENTS (or better 'eventing'), referred to in two
ways, objective and subjective.' (147)

'. . . in their own language, there are no verbs corresponding
to our **come** and go that mean simple and abstract motion, our
purely kinematic concept. The words in this case translated
come refer to the process of eventuating without calling it motion
—they are **eventuates to here** . . . or **eventuates from it** or **arrived**
which refers only to the terminal manifestation . . .' (60)

Hoijer (1954): 'The Navaho speaks of **actors** and **goals** (the terms
are inappropriate to Navaho), not as performers of actions or as
ones upon whom actions are performed, as in English, but as
entities linked to actions already defined in part as pertaining
especially to classes of beings.' (102)

Reichard (1949): 'The understanding of such verbs (i.e. verbs of
motion and action in Navaho) . . . will be greatly increased if the
verb be thought of as essentially emphasizing the kind of motion
. . . if one first personalizes the forms and moves out from the
subject instead of from the abstraction of impersonal motion, the
forms may make little sense and seem impossible to interpret.' (55)

Lee (1938): 'Category II (of the Wintu verbs) has reference to a state
of being in which the individual is not a free agent. In the statement

of this Category, attention is concentrated on the event and its ramifications, not on the actor.' (95)

Cassirer (1923): 'Der Beziehung des Vorgangs haftet hier zunächst weder die Beziehung auf einen Tätigen, noch die auf einen Leiden-den an: das Verbum konstatiert einfach den Eintritt des Vorgangs selbst, ohne ausdrücklich an die Energie eines Subjekt zu knüpfen oder die Beziehung zu dem Objekt, das von ihm betroffen wird, in der Verbalform selbst kenntlich zu machen.' (1954, 2nd edn: 220: referring to the Malaysian language)

There can naturally be delicate difference among the individual languages here discussed, but the recurrence of a series of clearly related notions like 'agent-orientated' vs. 'event-orientated', 'the agent in the foreground' vs. 'the agent suppressed' will readily be notice-able. These contrasting notions are also related to the problem of 'active' vs. 'passive', 'transitive' vs. 'intransitive' or of the 'nominal' nature of the verb (with a weakened agent in the possessive case), about which there is a large amount of literature.[22] We are not going into the discussion of these points.

3.8 TOWARDS A PSYCHOLINGUISTIC EXPLANATION

The two different types of linguistic organization we have identified presuppose different sets of principles at work behind them.

3.8.1 For the type of linguistic organization with a special emphasis on agentivity, which is here illustrated by English, we can offer an account like the following. The principles at work for it are: (a) The 'Concrete' over 'Abstract' Principle, (b) The 'Changed' over 'Un-changed' Principle, (c) The 'Animate' over 'Inanimate' Principle, (d) the Hypostatization of 'Abstract'.[23]

Of the three types of change we have been talking about, the change in locus is the most 'concrete'—'concrete' in the sense that the two terms (X and Y) involved in the change and the change itself are physically definable. This type of change is presumed to have served as a model for representing the other less concrete types of change (the 'Concrete' over 'Abstract' Principle). The change-in-locus patterns are fundamentally of two kinds: $X \rightarrow Y$ and $Y \leftarrow X$. Of the two, the former, in which X (i.e. something which changes) is the theme, is the commoner, the latter, as we have seen, usually having heavier restrictions imposed on its use (cp. 3.5.1) (the 'Changed' over 'Unchanged' Principle). If, however, Y happens to be animate (especially human), it is no longer simply a 'location'; it is reinterpreted as a '(prospective) possessor', which claims more of our attention and may consequently be placed in the thematic position (the 'Animate' over 'Inanimate' Principle). Moreover, Y is then a 'changed' term as well—'changed' as to whether or not it has X in its possession, so that the 'Changed' over 'Unchanged' Principle no longer applies. While the expression for the change in locus is X-orientated, that for the change in possessorship is decidedly Y-orientated. A further step is made when abstract notions are hypostatized[24] (e.g. 'a hit' or 'a pleasure' like 'a stone' or 'a book', and 'advice' or 'liberty' like 'water' or 'air') and are substituted for the concrete terms in the patterns for change in locus and in possessorship. Since the abstract notions are by nature imperceptible, the directionality of change is necessarily blurred in the representations of a change involving such terms—so that the contrast between the change in locus and that in possessorship comes to be neutralized (e.g. **John became old** and **John got old**, both admitting of a two-way interpretation: John $\rightleftarrows$ oldness; cp. 3.4.4). The process of 'incorporation' (e.g. BECOME (TO) DARK $\Rightarrow$ **darken**) is naturally common in the realization of the patterns involving abstract terms.

3.8.2 What are the corresponding principles which are working behind the other type of linguistic organization as represented by a language like Japanese? At least two of the four principles we have discussed in the previous section seem to remain: i.e. the 'Changed' over 'Unchanged' Principle and the 'Animate' over 'Inanimate' Principle. The former is manifested in the predominance of the X=theme pattern for the change in locus and the latter in the predominance of the Y=theme pattern for the change in possessorship. But while the 'Animate' over 'Inanimate' Principle seems to work in the English type of language to help develop the 'agent' vs. 'non-agent' contrast, as is manifested in the reinterpretation of Y as a proper grammatical subject which is predicated with a new HAVE-type of verb and in the correlated high frequency of the 'agent'-type of causative (i.e. W CAUSE [S]), the same principle in the Japanese type of language seems to work to help develop what may be called the 'experiencer' vs. 'non-experiencer' contrast, as is manifested in the simple allocation of Y (which still retains its 'goal' character) to the thematic position and in the correlated high frequency of the 'experiencer'-type of causative (i.e. W GET-HAVE [S]). The notion of the animate develops, in the English type of language, into that of the dynamic agent, positively causing a change in others; the same notion, in the Japanese type of language, however, tends to develop into that of the static experiencer, passively being affected by a change. Notice, however, that the staticity of the 'experiencer' notion does not imply that the 'animate' vs. 'inanimate' contrast is no longer significant. As is shown in 3.5.3, Japanese distinguishes between two verbs, IRU and ARU (both corresponding to the English verb be), in the 'state' expressions, the former applied to something animate (i.e. potential agent) and the latter to something inanimate. The two types of language only differ in the direction in which they have developed the 'animate' vs. 'inanimate' contrast.

Another point in which the two types of language show a marked contrast concerns the 'Concrete' over 'Abstract' Principle and its corollary, the Hypostatization of 'Abstract'. As seen from the comparative lack of freedom in transferring the verbs of motion or of personifying abstract notions, these do not seem to be particularly well applicable to Japanese. What replaces these in Japanese can perhaps be called the 'Process/State' over 'Participant' Principle, namely, that the role played by the participant in the event is subordinated to the process or state in which the participant is involved. The contrast between 'concrete' and 'abstract' still remains, but it now concerns the nature of the process or state as a whole rather than the nature of the participant. Thus the notions of the change in possessorship and of the possession (in which X, Y = concrete; $\rightarrow, \leftarrow, >, <$ = abstract) tend to merge with those of the change in condition and of the condition (because of the emphasis on $\rightarrow, \leftarrow, >, <$ rather than on X and Y).

There is clearly a correlation between the 'Process/State' over 'Participant' Principle and the development of the notion of the experiencer discussed in the preceding paragraph. In parallel, the development of the notion of the agent is clearly correlated with what we can call the 'Participant' over 'Process/State' Principle. The two principles perhaps represent two possible types of organization available to the human perception.

3.9 A POSSIBLE 'LOCUS'/'CONDITION' NEUTRALIZATION

We have seen in the above that there are two contrasting types of linguistic organization. It must not be thought, however, that these two types are so clearly separated as to be mutually exclusive of each other. There are events and situations which are susceptible of either type of organization equally well. In fact, it is perhaps for this reason that there emerge two such types of linguistic organization.

Ambiguity may arise in two ways: first, as to the contrast between 'concrete (motion or existence)' and 'abstract (motion or existence)' (i.e. the distinction among the change in locus, in possessorship and in condition or among spatial existence, possession and condition) and second, as the contrast between 'change' and 'state' in general.

3.9.1 The first point is already implied in the discussion we have made on the possibility of bidirectional interpretation for the change-in-possessorship or change-in-condition sentence with Y as theme (cp. 3.4.4). We have seen that in a typical change-in-possessorship sentence like **John got first prize** (John (Y) ← first prize (X)), there is a possibility of alternative interpretation, namely, John (Y) → first prize (X). But notice that while the former interpretation refers to the term X (i.e. first prize) as undergoing a change in possessorship, the latter refers to the term Y (i.e. John) as undergoing a change in condition, i.e. John changed from the condition of not having first prize to that of having one.

The creeping in of the notion of 'condition' is more extensively observed with the expression of state. Not only the patterns for possession, but also even those for spatial existence are affected. Thus a possessive sentence like **John has blue eyes** (John (Y) > blue eyes (X)) is readily reinterpreted as 'John is with blue eyes' (i.e. John (Y) < blue eyes (X)); similarly, even an existential sentence like **This room has two windows** (this room (Y) > two windows (X)) is reinterpretable as 'This room is with two windows' (i.e. this room (Y) < two windows (X)). Notice again that the alternative interpretation represents the situation as a 'condition' rather than as an instance of possession or spatial existence. Thus for the 'state' expressions, the notion of 'condition' invades not only that of 'possession' but also even that of 'spatial existence'.

3.9.2 Just as there is a possibility of ambiguity among the three types of change and among the three types of state, so the distinction between the two major categories we have been assuming as fundamental, namely, 'change' and 'state', is not an absolute one. Here ambiguity arises whenever either or both of the two terms, X and Y, represent something non-discrete. First, consider the following sentences:

49. An apple drops to the ground.
50. The ivy grows to the top of the wall.
51. The water flows into the basin.
52. The light comes into the room.

As we come down from (49) to (52), the body in motion (i.e. X) becomes less discrete; correspondingly, we notice a gradual shift from the notion of the change in locus through that of the change in condition to that of the condition or state. Similarly, compare the following:

53. The balloon descends on to the ground.
54. The moon rises.
55. The car moves on.

Sentence (53), like (49), refers to a specific non-discrete goal (Y). Sentence (54) refers to an upward movement, but without any specific goal, the goal being here conceived of as a continuum. The extreme case of a non-discrete goal is represented by a non-directed motion as in (55). A non-directed motion is easily associated with the notion of continuation at a constant pace, and to the extent that it lacks a change in pace, it can be taken as a state[25] (cp. 3.6.1).

When a continuum makes a non-directed motion, the whole picture is quite close to that of a state:

56. The fog flows over the field.
57. The water spreads over the whole area.
58. The wind blows through the wood.

It is but a step from a sentence like (57) to (59):

59. The odour pervades the whole area.

Abstract notions are by nature not discrete. But for the very reason that they are imperceptible, they are at the same time also susceptible of being hypostatized. It is expected that hypostatization is a commoner phenomenon in a language which tends to give prominence to the participant than in one in which the notion of the event as a whole is emphasized. One may recall Whorf's characterization of the Hopi notion of time—'getting later and later', which he contrasts with the SAE notion of time as something which can be beautifully segmented. The image of an amorphous fluid will be appropriate to the former conception.

3.10 CONCLUDING REMARKS

We have started with a would-be localist assumption that all the linguistic expressions of change and state are modelled after those of the most concrete types of change and state, i.e. motion and spatial existence. It has been made clear in the foregoing discussion that

there is certainly a set of common underlying patterns for the
linguistic representation of 'change' and 'state', that these patterns
can very closely be approximated to those for representing motion
and spatial existence, but that at the same time the claim of universal priority of the localistic notions does not hold. The contrast
between 'concrete (motion or existence)' and 'abstract (motion
or existence)' and also the one between 'change' and 'state' in
general are by no means so simplistic as might be imagined. Thus
we have seen how the notion of 'spatial existence' is easily reinterpreted as 'condition'. The notion of 'change in locus' appears somewhat more secure, but against it are ranked the other two types of
change as well as all the three types of state. The notion is in fact
partly invaded by the possibility of a non-directed type of motion
being interpreted as a 'condition'.

We are not going to involve ourselves here in the discussion as to
which of the two types of linguistic organization is 'more natural'
or whether these two types can be correlated with such character-
izations as the 'synthetic' vs. 'analytic' way of thinking, the 'positive'
vs. 'negative' pattern of behaviour, the 'man-oriented' vs. 'nature-
oriented' type of philosophy, the 'individualistic' vs. 'totalistic'
social organization, etc. To do so would require more sophisticated
psychological inquiries and philosophical considerations than I am
prepared to do now.[26] If, however, it is true, as some linguists
suggest, that the kind of language that we find Indo-European
today is really a later development and that in its early stages it had
much more of the other type of linguistic organization, then one
may perhaps be allowed to conjecture that there must have been
behind the remarkable typological change it has undergone something—something which perhaps we may call a strong interest or
even belief in the potentiality of man.

NOTES

1. A good discussion of the localist theory of case is found in Hjelmslev
   (1935:36-61).
2. Although the illustration is here limited to English, there are languages in
   which the presumed underlying patterns come out more 'transparent'
   than in the case of English. In Japanese, for example, the sentences equivalent to (33), (34), (35), (36) and (38) have the goal (or contiguity)
   marker realized as a surface form.
3. In the following, the focus of the discussion will be laid on the representation
   of 'change' rather than 'state' because of its greater relevance to our theme.
   For a fuller discussion of the point, see Ikegami (1973) and Ikegami
   (1975:329-438).

4. I am fully aware of different definitions proposed for the term 'theme': cp. Firbas (1966), Halliday (1970:353-60) and also Gruber (1965:47-53) and Jackendoff (29). The Gruber-Jackendoff notion of the theme is likely to coincide with what I refer to by X in this paper. My use of the term is perhaps closest to that of Halliday, who distinguishes the 'theme'-'rheme' relation from the 'given'-'new' relation. Two points, however, must be noted with regard to the term 'sentence-initial' position. First, our consideration of 'theme' vs. 'non-theme' distinction is limited to the two elements, X and Y, as constituents of underlying abstract patterns. In actual surface sentences, it may very well be that some adverbial elements occupy the 'sentence-initial' position. Second, the notion of 'sentence-initial' position is also applied in this paper to an S (a structural unit realizable as a surface sentence) embedded in the underlying abstract pattern, so that we will talk about the realization of an X=theme pattern for an expression like **send a letter to John** (i.e. CAUSE [a letter (X) → John (Y)]) or of a Y=theme pattern for an expression like **send John a letter** (i.e. CAUSE [John (Y) ← a letter (X)]).

5. The use of capitals in the representation of structural patterns is to indicate that the forms given are 'idealized' verbs which may be realized as more than one separate surface verb with its specific restrictions on use.

6. The preferential choice between the patterns, WITH Y BE X and Y HAVE X, has traditionally been noted as a contrast between 'BE-language' and 'HAVE-language'. It will also be interesting to consider the notions of 'intrinsic' and 'extrinsic' possession in relation to these two patterns (cp. Benveniste:1960).

7. We will again not be going into an interesting discussion of a possibility of reducing the 'non-causative' to the causative by considering the former as a special case of the latter, namely, 'self-causation' (e.g. **John ran to the station** = John CAUSE [self → the station]). See Ikegami 91973:28-33), Ikegami (1975:357-62).

8. I leave open the question how much the notion of 'experiencer' as defined in this way coincides with that of Fillmore's 'experiencer'.

9. The term 'incorporation' is due to Gruber (1965). Gruber, for example, describes the verb **cross** as being derived from the 'incorporation' of ACROSS into GO.

10. In relation to the contrast between the patterns, GIVE Y X (or alternatively, GIVE TO Y X) and PROVIDE Y WITH X, it will be interesting to consider Weisgerber's distinction between what he calls, 'Mensch im Dativ' and 'Mensch im Akkusativ'. Cp. 'Es scheint, dass in die heutigen deutschen Sprache einer Verfahrensweise verstärktes Gewicht zukommt, die Personen, die in ein Geschehen einbezogen sind, in die sprachliche Rolle des Akkusativobjekts bringt' (1958;193). Weisgerber here refers to the increasing use of the PROVIDE Y (accusative) WITH X pattern (e.g. **einen mit etwas beliefern**) as against the GIVE (TO) Y (dative) X pattern (e.g. **einem etwas liefern**). According to him, 'im Akkusativobjekt ist der Mensch . . . Objekt im vollen Sinne. Im Dativ bleibt der Mensch "sinngebende Person" . . . Im Dativ ist der Mensch Mittelpunkt des Geschehens, wird er als Person zur Geltung gebracht; im Akkusativ wird er "erfasst", wird er Gegenstand einer geistigen Machtausübung' (200). If we think, as will be discussed in the present paper, that the pattern, PROVIDE Y WITH X (= CAUSE [Y BECOME WITH X]), is a way of representing a change in possessorship

as if it were a change in condition and that the notion of agentivity (which characterizes the animate, and especially the human, being) becomes less conspicuous in the change in condition, Weisgerber's intuitive judgement seems to be quite to the point.

11. For a fuller discussion of the scheme as a possible framework for contrastive analysis, see Ikegami (1976b).

12. Ga, o, e, and ni are all 'postpositions'. Ga is the subject marker, o the object marker, e a goal marker, and ni a location marker. ni, however, is often transferred as a goal marker.

13. However, it seems to be reasonable to represent the different behaviours of verbs like hit and open in terms of the contrast, namely,

John hit the door.   'John DO hitting (X) TO the door (Y)'
John CAUSE [hitting $(X) \to$ the door (Y)]

John opened the door.   'John MAKE the door (Y) WITH openness (X)'
John CAUSE [the door $(Y) \to$ openness (X)]

It is often claimed that the hit-type transitive verbs cannot be paraphrased as causatives, but the present analysis implies that this is by no means the case and that the difference consists in the different thematization as regards X and Y in the embedded structure dominated by CAUSE.

14. For a fuller discussion, see Ikegami (1976a).

15. $\overline{Y}$ means the complement of Y. The equivalence, FROM $Y =$ TO $\overline{Y}$ has been suggested by Gruber (1965:68).

16. The same account applies to the verbs referring to 'expanding', 'shrinking', 'stretching', etc., which stand midway between the verbs of motion and those of change in condition. Thus the English expression, **expand to a huge ball**, will have to be phrased in Japanese as something like 'expand and become a huge ball' or 'expand till it becomes a huge ball'.

17. Cp. Bally (1926:75: referring to a change from **Mihi sunt capilli nigri** to **J'ai les cheveux noirs** and similar instances): 'Le changement général a consisté à renverser certains types de phrases comportant un datif de participation, **de manière que la personne intéressée devînt sujet de la phrase**.'; Brinkmann (1959:180–01: referring to an alternation between **Hast du es warm?** and **Ist es bei dir warm?** and similar instances): 'In allen diesen und den verwandten Fällen gibt "haben" dem Sprecher die Möglichkeit, den Menschen selber als Subjekt in den Mittelpunkt zu rücken. . . . Der "haben"-Satz erlaubt eine persönliche Perspektive.'

18. The possibility of adding a phrase like **for her** without making the sentence semantically redundant testifies to the fact that **Mary** in such a sentence is no longer an exponent of a mere affected one.

19. Compare, in this connection, Seiler's notion of 'possessor of an act', although it does not entirely coincide with the notion of 'experiencer' as expounded in this paper: ' "Possessor of an act" conveys the idea that someone is associated with an ACT in a way in which neither the AGENT nor the OBJECT is associated. I might also say that the POSSESSOR is credited with the ACT, . . .' (1973:837)

20. The type of Japanese expression I have in mind is: X **ni okase-rare-mashite-wa**, Y **ni nara-re-mashita**—an extremely respectful way of saying talking about X's act (Y). The use of the verbal suffix **-(ra)reru**, also commonly employed as a (quasi-)passive marker, in the honorific language also serves the same purpose of suppressing the agentivity. Outside the honorofic

language, the verb **naru** ('to become') is very commonly used, serving to give the expression a peculiar impersonal tone. Thus instead of saying (the equivalent of) 'The meeting has been cancelled' or 'We are getting married next month', people often prefer to say something like 'the meeting has "become" to cancellation' or '(It) has "become" that we are getting married next month'.

21. Herrfahrdt's examples for 'Erlebnissatz' are **es regnet, es ist kalt.** An example of 'Aussagesatz' is **der Hund ist ein Säugetier.**

22. The contrast was characterized by Schuchardt (1895:3) as 'es wird von mir gesehen' vs. 'es wird mir sichtbar'.

23. I assume that these 'principles' can be justified on independent grounds without referring to what happens in language. Otherwise, the whole argument would fall in the same vicious circle for which the Sapir-Whorf hypothesis is often criticized.

24. 'Personification' of abstract notions seems to be a much more common phenomenon in a language like English than Japanese. This is well expected, because personification will be so much the easier the more firmly established are the structural patterns for agent-orientated expressions.

25. This is where the notion of 'duration' comes in. It partakes both of the property of 'change' and of that of 'state'. Consider also in this connection the two contrasting notions of 'time' as described by Gonda: 'Whereas we regard time as a stream or straight line, as a regular succession of single, unique, and irrevocable moments, without beginning in the past and without end in the future, the primitive experiences it as duration or as periodical recurrence, conceiving it as a cycle, as something that can return, as something that can be renewed' (1956:25-6). The two notions of time may be compared to the two types of 'motion'—one represented by 'going', 'travelling', 'running', 'walking', 'creeping', etc. and the other represented by 'turning (of a disc)', 'shaking (of a tuning fork)', 'expanding (of a piece of metal)', 'shrinking (of a balloon)', etc. Notice that the second type of 'motion' is not so much a change in locus, as the first type of motion is, as a change in condition or even a condition.

26. There is no lack of interesting ideas and suggestions in the writings of comparative culture with which we can start a fruitful discussion in this line. (See, for example, Nakamura (1962), to which the following account owes considerably.) One of the recurrent themes is the contrast between the 'Western' notion of the nature as opposed to man and the Japanese notion of the nature as incorporating man. From this comes the contrast between the notion of culture as something produced *by* man through his working on the nature and the notion of culture as nature manifesting itself *through* man. Thus in any art or discipline, whether it be the tea ceremony, flower arrangement, Zen Buddhism, Haiku poems, judo or any of the traditional kind of sculpture, painting, dancing, fencing, swimming, etc., what is required of one newly to be initiated is to suppress (or 'kill') himself and let himself be where 'nature' would take him. This tendency of becoming one with 'nature', of submerging oneself in 'nature', is also said to be manifested as the comparative readiness with which the Japanese accept the reality and the concomitant unwillingness to interrupt or disturb the 'smooth flowing' of the event. Thus politically and socially, the notion of the 'free individual' acting on his own has never been well developed in Japan. An acute foreign observer, borrowing Bergson's words, talks about 'that "constant force of direction that is to the soul what gravity is to the

bodies'', assuring cohesion of the group by inclining individual wills in the same direction and thus creating "an order dictated by impersonal requirements" ' (Singer 1973:73). 'To move forward in silence and to establish directions of action without being aware of doing so are inherent aspects of the Japanese character' (Ben-Dasan 1972:69). It is recalled that a singularly tight national unity under the emperor and an equally tight family unity under the father were undeniable characteristics of the traditional Japanese society. Psychologically, maintaining good human relations ('not hurting the feelings of others') is valued higher than asserting oneself, and the behaviour of the Japanese is commented on by Westerners as 'polite', 'unfathomable', 'unreliable' or even 'deceptive', as the case may be. (For a full discussion of these and other related points, readers are referred to Ikegami (forthcoming) and the Introduction in the same volume.)

BIBLIOGRAPHY

Bally, Charles (1926), 'L'expression des idées de sphère personnelle et de solidarité dans les langues indo-européennes', in *Festschrift for Louis Gauchat*, 68-78, Aarau, Verlag H. R. Sauerländer & Co.

Ben-Dasan, Isaiah (1972), *The Japanese and the Jews*, translated by Richard L. Gage, New York, Weatherhill.

Benveniste, Emil (1960), 'Être et avoir dan leurs fonctions linguistiques', *Bulletin de la Société Linguistique de Paris*, 55; 113-34. (Also in *Problèmes de linguistique générale*, Paris, Gallimard, 1966: 187-207.)

Brinkmann, Hennig (1959), 'Die "HABEN" Perfektive im Deutschen', in Helmut Gipper (ed.), *Sprache—Schlüssel zur Welt, Festschrift für Leo Weisgerber*, Düsseldorf, Schwann, 176-94.

Cassirer, Ernst (1923, 1954, 2nd edn), *Philosophie der symbolischen Formen: Erster Teil, Die Sprache*, Oxford, Bruno Cassirer.

Finck, F. N. (1909), *Die Haupttypen des Sprachbaus*, Leipzig, Teubner.

Firbas, Jan (1966), 'On defining the theme in functional sentence perspective', *Travaux linguistiques de Prague*, 1; 267-80.

Gonda, J. (1956), *The Character of the Indo-European Moods: with Special Regard to Greek and Sanskrit*, Wiesbaden, Otto Harrassowitz.

Gruber, Jeffrey S. (1965), 'Studies in lexical relations', in *Lexical Structures in Syntax and Semantics* (1976), Amsterdam: North-Holland.

Halliday, Michael A. K. (1970), 'Functional diversity in language as seen from a consideration of modality and mood in English', *Foundations of Language*, 6, 322-61.

Hartmann, Hans (1954), *Das passiv. Eine Studie zur Geistesgeschichte der Kelten, Italiker und Arier*, Heidelberg, Carl Winter.

Hartmann, Peter (1954), *Einige Grundzüge des japanischen Sprachbaues*, Heidelberg. Carl Winter.

Hartung, Johann A. (1831), *Ueber die Casus, ihre Bildung und Bedeutung, in der griechischen und lateinischen Sprache*, Erlangen, J. J. Palm und Ernst Enke.

Herrfahrdt, H. (1938), 'Die innere Sprachform des Japanischen im Vergleich mit der indogermanischen Sprachen', in *Wörter und Sachen*, 19 (Neue Folge, Band 1), 165-76.

Hjelmslev, L. (1935, 1937), 'La catégorie des cas. Étude de grammaire générale',

Acta Jutlandica, 7, 1, i-xii, 1-184; 9, 2, i-vii, 1-78. (Also reprinted in München, Wilhelm Fink.)

Hockett, C. (1954), 'Chinese versus English: an exploration of the Whorfian hypothesis', in Hoijer (ed.) (1954: 106-26).

Hoijer, H. (1954), 'The Sapir-Whorf hypothesis', in Hoijer (ed.) (1954: 92-105).

Hoijer, H. (ed.) (1954), *Language in culture*, Chicago, University Press.

Ikegami, Y. (1970), *The Semological Structure of the English Verbs of Motion*, Tokyo, Sanseido.

Ikegami, Y. (1973), 'A set of basic patterns for the semantic structure of the verb', *Linguistics*, 170, 31-44.

Ikegami, Y. (1975), *Imiron* (= *Semantics*), Tokyo, Taishukan.

Ikegami, Y. (1976a), 'Syntactic structure and the underlying semantic patterns: a localist hypothesis', *Linguistics*, 170, 31-44.

Ikegami, Y. (1976b), 'A localist hypothesis as a framework for contrastive linguistics', *Folia Linguistica*, IX-1-4, 59-71.

Ikegami, Y. (1977), 'A localist theory and the structure of text', in G. Nickel (ed.), *Proceedings of the Fourth International Congress of Applied Linguistics*, Stuttgart, Hochschulverlag, 339-48.

Ikegami, Y. (1978), 'A linguistic model for narrative analysis', in M. Loflin and J. Silverberg (eds), *Discourse and Inference in Cognitive Anthropology*, The Hague, Mouton, 111-34.

Ikegami, Y. (forthcoming), 'The World of Continuum: Japanese as "BE- and BECOME-language"', in Y. Ikegami (ed.), *The Empire of Signs*, Amsterdam, John Benjamins.

Jackendoff, R. S. (1972), *Semantic interpretation in generative grammar*, Cambridge, Mass., MIT Press.

Lee, D. (1939), 'Conceptual implications of an Indian language', *Philosophy of Science*, 5, 89-102.

Martinet, André (1958), 'La construction ergative et les structures élémentaires de l'énoncé', *Journal de psychologie*, 55, 377-92. (Also in *La linguistique synchronique*, Paris, Universitaires de France, 1965, 206-22).

Nakamura, Hajime (1962), *Tooyoojinno shii-hoohoo* (= *The Oriental way of thinking*), Tokyo, Shunjuusha.

Reichard, Gladys A. (1949), 'The character of the Navaho verb stem', *Word*, 5, 55-76.

Sakuma, Kanae (1941), *Nihongo no Tokushitsu* (= *Some characteristics of the Japanese language*), Tokyo, Ikuei-Shoin.

Seiler, Hansjakob (1973), 'On the semantico-syntactic configuration "possessor of an act"', in *Issues in Linguistics: Papers in Honor of Henry and Renée Kahane*, Urbana, University of Illinois Press, 836-53.

Singer, Kurt (1973), *Mirror, Sword and Jewel: a Study of Japanese Characteristics*, edited with an introduction by Richard Storry, London, Croom Helm.

Weisgerber, Leo (1958), 'Der Mensch im Akkusative', *Wirkendes Wort*, 8, 193-205.

Weisgerber, Leo (1973), 'Die Welt im Passive"', in *Die Wissenschaft von deutschen Sprache und Dichtung: Methoden, Problem, Aufgabe: Festschirft für Friedrich Mauer*, Stuttgard, Ernst Klett, 25-59.

Whorf, Benjamin L. (1956), *Language, Thought and Reality*, edited by John B. Carroll, Cambridge, Mass., MIT Press.

Wüllner, Franz (1827), *Die Bedeutung der sprachlichen Casus und Modi*, Münster, Verlag in der Coppenrathschen Buch- und Kunsthandlung.

4 Some speculations on language contact in a wider setting

Jeffrey Ellis
University of Aston, Birmingham, UK

4.1 INTRODUCTION

My title is deliberately vague and tentative. At the heart of the subject lies the question: what light is thrown on the relation between language and culture (and general and social semiotic) by the contact relations between languages and cultures? But this question is bound up with a multitude of interrelated questions, which can be attacked only at limited points in limited samples of topics and data.

Such topics will include attempts to relate not just Balkan (Ellis 1963a, 1966d, 1967), West African (Ellis 1971a), or other areal convergence (Ellis 1965a and 1966a) but language contact in general (Ellis 1965a, 1966a, Ellis forthcoming a, §3.2) with linguistic function (Ellis forthcoming b and c) and extra-linguistic environment and culture. It is perhaps in some senses premature to try to relate such generalized but complex diachronic, or panchronic, considerations to the subject of this symposium, which most contributions are treating descriptively within one language or culture. The immediate need for research on languages in contact is precisely their more delicate *linguistic* description. For a linguist at this stage to attempt to go beyond this can only be characterized as speculation. However, if these speculations should prove of any interest to a general semiotic audience, the feedback could be of considerable value to the linguistics of language contact in providing it with the wider stimulus that the disciplines making up a general semiotic audience can give.

We may classify language contact as follows, but remembering that the integration of these categories into an overall drawing together of the world's languages, dialects and language varieties has been shown—by Becker, Weinreich, and others—to be a fruitful and desirable goal even if not yet worked out in detail.

As regards the descriptive linguistic effects of contact: at one end we have small-scale borrowing of items, usually in this case at the lexical level; at the other end we have the creation of new languages, pidgins or creoles, involving all linguistic levels; in between (Georgiev 1966:6) we have the modification of languages into members of *Sprachbünde* or convergence areas, as regards the phonological, syntactical or phraseological levels as well as the lexical. (The term 'phraseological level' is an *ad hoc* designation of something to which I shall return.)

As regards the sociolinguistic conditions of contact, various terminologies have been proposed, with terms like the traditional 'substratum', to which 'superstratum' and 'adstratum' have been added, or Ferguson's 'superposition'—of a completely distinct language in what Kloss terms 'out-diglossia' or of a related language-variety in his 'in-diglossia'.

These concepts are of importance when we come to distinguish more precisely within the category I have referred to as *Sprachbund* or convergence area, as well as to re-unite pidgins and creoles with other kinds of language contact, but first I ought to emphasize that from the linguistic point of view the primary datum is what I have called the descriptive linguistic effects of contact, which are with us in the observable features of languages living or recorded, when the extra-linguistic contacts that resulted in them *may* be lost in the mists of history or prehistory.

The Balkan languages, for example, indisputably display a complex array of linguistic features in common between various combinations of them, but the extra-linguistic reasons for these are still in dispute. Or to take such examples a step further, the languages of Southern Ghana exhibit a somewhat comparable community of features; unlike the Balkan languages these are all relatively closely related genetically, in the Kwa[1] branch of the Niger-Congo family, but again unlike the Balkan languages (both Indo-European and Turkic), for a number of reasons including paucity of historical records the comparative philology of this family is at a rudimentary stage, so that the disentangling of areal convergence from original genetic relationship is not as straightforward, to say the least.

Or again, it is a fact that European languages share the formation of many items of vocabulary that Chinese, for example (to name another principal civilization and *Kultursprache* of the world), forms in some other way;[2] it is a speculation, of the most dubious kind, when Lewy (1942) attributes more 'abstraction' to western than eastern Eurasian languages.

In proceeding from the linguistic data to their possible relations to a wider semiotic framework, I will touch on a few examples under the following two sets of headings: considerations of language-contact (1-5 below) and general semiotic and cultural considerations (a-g below).

The 'facts' of descriptive linguistics, historical linguistics, and the sociolinguistics of who speaks what (institutional linguistics) may be classified into:

1. Language contact as a whole, which is (and has been) the rule, not the exception (cp. Fishman: 'interference' is a misnomer).
2. In particular, societal bilingualism (especially Ferguson's 'super-position', Kloss's 'out-diglossia'), which is inextricably inter-dependent with register.
3. *Sprachbünde* in Becker's sense, which form a network of over-lapping, and historically shifting, groupings throughout the civilized world (mainly lexical (and phraseological); also the graphic level).
4. *Sprachbund* in the Balkan sense, which is a linguistically far-reaching (at all levels) result of past contacts, not always historically deter-minable.
5. Pidgins and creoles, which are a particular case of the contact generality (1 and 2 above) and of *Sprachbund* (Weinreich 1958, Becker; see 4.6.1).

Aspects of wider setting, which can be used to cross-classify these five, include:

a. Language functions and the grammatical level.
b. The sociolinguistics of the relation between language and social setting (sociological linguistics, linguistic sociology).
c. 'Culture contact', including oral and other literature, proverbs, metaphor, etc. (See 4.4.2.)
d. Linguistic relativity (Sapir-Whorf hypothesis), e.g. the question of 'to be'.
e. 'Register networks' (cp. Fawcett).
f. Semiotic methodology.
g. 'Interlanguage', information retrieval theory, and other applica-tions.

In this chapter examples are given for about half the 5 X 7 cells in this matrix, including at least one example of each row and each column, as shown in Figure 4.1.

4.2 GENERAL LANGUAGE–CULTURE CONTACT

4.2.1 Language contact as a whole and language functions

For a general account of language functions (ideational (experiential and logical), interpersonal, textual) in linguistic theory see Halliday

		functions	sociolinguistic	culture	relativity	register networks	semiotic	interlanguage
		a	b	c	d	e	f	g
general	1	4.2.1		4.2.3	4.2.1			
bilingualism	2	4.2.1	4.3.1	4.3.2	4.2.1	4.3.3.	4.3.3	
Becker-type	3		4.4.1	4.4.2	4.4.3		4.4.2	
Balkan-type	4	4.5.1		4.5.2	4.5.3			4.5.4
pidgins	5	4.6.2			4.6.3	4.6.4		

Fig. 4.1 Matrix of topics

1970, 1974, and 1977, Ellis 1978, forthcoming b and c. The functions are involved in various ways in the different kinds of language contact.

Verbs of 'being', to be discussed more fully under 4.6.3, illustrate the textual function (specifically, informational structuring[3])[4] as well as the experiential.

For example, the English use (textual, informational) of it's . . . that . . . is notoriously more extensive (in elements thematized, e.g. it's singing he is) in Irish English (i.e. in the 'more Irish' varieties, cp. Gumperz, quoting Macnamara, quoted in Ellis forthcoming §3.4), under the influence of the use of is in Irish (e.g. is thíos atá sé, 'it's below that he is').

The experiential distinction of Irish bíonn, 'be habitually' (from tá, 'be temporarily', see 4.5.1) is represented in Irish English by do be, generalized from the rare English negative or interrogative doesn't be, does he be? (imperative don't be is not limited to habitual meaning).

For examples of the interpersonal and logical functions see 4.5.1, 4.6.2.

4.2.2 Culture contact in general

On the question of correlation between language contact and culture contact, or, more descriptively, *Sprachbund* and *cultural* ties, it becomes essential to refine the concept of *Sprachbund*. For Becker (1948: 5, 23–9) languages form a *Sprachbund* if one of them, the *Meistersprache*, (ibid.: 20, 53), is a source for the development of the others' expression of what they have culturally in common, by the borrowing of what Hill (1958: 447) calls 'new lexicon',[5] either directly or by calquing, or of turns of phrase by calquing of phraseology (Becker 1948:83).[6] (This corresponds to Bloomfield's 'cultural borrowing', but elsewhere we may find trouble in the application of this term, when culture includes intimate culture in the sense of his 'intimate borrowing', cp. Becker, 1948: 29–41.) If this is the minimum condition for a *Sprachbund*, it is apparent that any language outside a primitive community (cp. n.5) will belong to at least one *Sprachbund*, and Becker's thesis is one of the kind familiar in the history of science that are in themselves not new, yet their systematic enunciation marks a turning-point in the development of ideas. The idea needed breaking down that languages in their relation to cultures are self-contained *vis-à-vis* other languages, and Becker did this, and did it more comprehensively than for example contemporaries of his to be referred to under 4.4.3 (cp. Becker 1948: 14).

The pre-Becker use (cp. Becker 1948: 20, 23, 25) of the term *Sprachbund*, also termed linguistic convergence area (Ellis 1963a), is reserved for languages that have through long and intimate contacts become partially assimilated to each other at more levels than Becker's *Sprachbünde*, and indeed not necessarily in 'new lexicon' (where they may belong to different Becker-*Sprachbünde*), but, in the case of the Balkan languages for example, very much in everyday (intimate) phraseology, along with metaphor, proverbs and oral literature forms and themes (cp. Sandfeld 1930; Ure 1963).

An example of Becker's categories (my example using his general terms, but cp. Becker 1948: 45, 37 ff.): Hindi-Urdu, genetically related to Sanskrit, belongs historically to the Persian-*Meistersprache Unterbund* of the Islamic *Sprachbund, Meistersprache* Arabic, to which Urdu still belongs, while Hindi belongs to the Sanskrit *Sprachbund*.

4.2.3 Language contact as a whole and culture contact

Because language and culture (however else they may agree or differ, have or have not similar semiotics) have different rates of change and ways of changing, it is not always obvious that there is a basic and long-term correspondence between a *continuum* of culture or cultures over most of the present world (with cultural traits constituting what might be termed isoeths) and a continuum of languages, as regards various features, detailed in 4.1 (with interlingual isoglosses, cp. Ellis 1966c: 137).

Within each of these continua there are nodal points of discontinuity of various kinds and varying degree, and under this head also belongs the general point of language–culture relationship (in the sense of whether the correspondence of languages and cultures is one-to-one[7]) that discontinuities between languages and between cultures are not always the same, and this would seem to have implications for analysis of the general relation between a single language and culture.

For example, a schematic representation of the languages and cultures of contemporary Ghana (as distinct from a developing society with an 'indigenous' official national language like Swahili) would look like this (Figure 4.2).

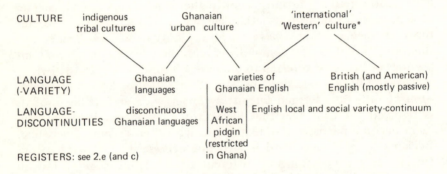

Fig. 4.2 Culture and language in Ghana

Note: This corresponds in part of its printed material aspect to Ferguson's third (and fourth) degrees of written language use, possessed by only a few of the world's languages, namely a full range of publication (and translation from other degree 3, and other, languages) on the physical sciences, etc.

Many things are left out of this diagram, e.g. discrimination between Ghanaian languages that are koines in urban culture, or other more delicate 'joins' between cultures and particular languages or language varieties.[8]

The representation of language–discontinuities assumes the common opinion of (socio)linguists that West African pidgin and English are not only different languages but linguistically discontinuous, though this demands more research (cp. Ellis forthcoming a, §3, on post-creole and 'post-pidgin' communities).

Note that the diagram does not accompany language–discontinuities with 'culture–discontinuities' or -overlaps or -subordinations, but see 4.3.2 below.

4.3 BILINGUALISM

4.3.1 Bilingualism and social setting

One feature of Ghanaian urban culture is the practice of inscribing short texts ('mottoes, proverbs, epigraphs and other strange devices', Field 1960: 134) on the passenger lorries that are a feature of West African (anglophone[9]) interurban economy ('Ordinary Ghana people, in passenger lorries, probably travel more often, faster, farther and lighter than any other people in the world', Field ibid.: 134).

Linguistically these are as often as not in some variety of English, ranging, in their degree of difference from British English, from **God dey** (for **dey** see 4.6.3), Field ibid.; 142 **God is**, or **Skin pain**, to **All the world is a stage**, where the additional syllable taking the poetry out of Shakespeare, to me, is characteristic of 'type 2' (Criper 1971 a and b) and below Ghanaian English grammar of intonation (without British English weak forms) (cp. Schneider 1966: 235-7).

Culturally, according to Field (ibid.: 134-5), they usually express the drivers' or owners' psychological insecurity and tension:

the driver is acutely conscious of himself as an object of envy, . . . the buying of lorries is one of the major outlets of rural wealth . . . In the choice of these inscriptions the driver unconsciously reveals his dominant attitude, and pre-occupations, sentiments and character-traits. Many of the same inscriptions that are painted on lorries are also painted on the outsides of houses, particularly new or newly inherited ones. [I have also seen biblical references, i.e. chapter and verse numbers without text, on vending kiosks.—J.E.] The lorry-drivers' attitudes are in fact the normal ones, enunciated with rather more than normal clarity and trenchancy.

Field lists 144 examples, in English or a Ghanaian language, with 'the meaning as explained by the driver or other informant', e.g. (p. 142, no. 100) **God is** means 'Through God I have a lorry.'

4.3.2 Bilingualism and culture contact

Ure (1974) describes and classifies various kinds of mixing and switching between languages, including 'mixed speech' in the sense of 'a type of language patterning that draws upon the structures as well as the lexis of the two languages and switches from one language to another regularly within a text, often a number of times within a single sentence' and 'the regular occurrence among the elite in many developing nations of a language patterning of this type where the local languages are mixed with the dominant international or post-colonial language of the locality' (cp. Ellis 1976 on the place of these data in the linguistics of 'mixed texts', Hill 1958: 450).

As 'a register in the community's register range, learnt as a part of linguistic socialization' (Ure 1974), at least in contemporary developing countries[10] like Ghana (Ure also has historical examples), on both linguistic and sociolinguistic criteria,[11] mixed speech belongs to the native-language part of the register-range (cp. Ellis forthcoming a §3.21).

In relating this linguistic phenomenon to culture we have a particular case of the question touched on under 4.2.2: how far is multilingualism accompanied by multiculturalism? Ure suggests that in stating the cultural correlate of mixed speech we might distinguish between a total culture, which may or may not be a culture-complex, and the cultures which are the elements in a culture-complex, whether or not they also exist independently. But the correspondence with cultures is not of the linguistic components (items, exponents of categories[12]) mixed—cp. Ure 1974: 'rather than to try to account in sociolinguistic terms for each change every few seconds. . . . mixed is a feature of social, not individual language behaviour . . .'. As regards mixed speech as a whole in my diagram (Fig. 4.2) of Ghanaian cultures and languages (and in 4.3.3, register networks) mixed speech belongs in the section 'indigenous Ghanaian languages', e.g. Akan, cultural section 'urban culture' (at its 'international culture' end).

4.3.3 Bilingualism and register networks, semiotic methodology

The principle of register networks is discussed in Fawcett 1980. As a system network a register network exhibits the register systems of the unit text (Halliday 1977 §§3.2, 4.2).

One relation between the two languages in contact, English and a Ghanaian language, is shown by the register networks in Ure 1975 for British English, Ghanaian English (cp. Ure 1970) and a Ghanaian language (Akan; also data for Ewe and Ga).

These differ from normal system networks in not being ordered by features in the most economical arrangement but by the degree of distinctness of realization of register-difference by grammar-lexis ratio, indicated numerically by figures for the sample. (For the grammar-lexis ratio method of register-discrimination see Ure 1971.)

They suggest fairly subtle differences, and resemblances, between the two kinds of English and between the two languages in Ghanaian bilingualism, as regards taxonomy of mode (spoken/written; dialogue/monologue) and social role (e.g. action(immediate/non-immediate)/secondary (Ure 1969); Akan 'useful'/'polished', including a distinction between modern prose and traditional stories etc. which correlates with one made elsewhere (Ellis 1971c, 1978, Ellis and Boadi 1969: 61–2), on other grounds, of two varieties of Akan, 'traditional registers' and other (partly English-influenced) registers).

4.4 BECKER-TYPE *SPRACHBÜNDE*

4.4.1 *Sprachbund* (Becker) and social setting

The conception of *Sprachbund* in Becker's sense might be said to correspond in the linguistic sphere to the conception in the cultural, or specifically geopolitical, sphere, of the international metropolis (the number of these being reduced to very few in our present world), such as New York, Paris, Peking. This conception is of course open to objections of being unsubstantiated scientifically, speculative in a bad sense, and so on. In any case, shifts in *Sprachbund* patterns would clearly lag far behind those in metropolis-orientation, if one were to recognize such a thing. But on the other hand there is a seeming correspondence with Becker's (1948: 15) characterization of his *Sprachbund* relations as 'jumping between centres, not wavelike' as distinct from Balkan-type *Sprachbund* relations, which are between groupings of local dialects of the languages (and for Becker (23 ff.) Balkan is an *Unterbund*).

4.4.2 *Sprachbund* (Becker) and culture contact; semiotic methodology

An obvious feature of Becker's *Sprachbünde* outside the aspects of language we shall otherwise be concerned with, but within the total scheme of linguistic levels, is the writing system (Becker 1948: 69 ff.); and the sharing of a writing system by languages whose link is not genetic relation or linguistic type but *Bund*-membership is clearly the reason for the well-known (e.g. Lyons 1968: 39) phenomenon of languages using a linguistically inappropriate writing system. Examples are Turkish before Atatürk initiated what might be described as anti-*Meistersprache* action[13] or Japanese,[14] a less simple example since the complexity of kanamajiri as a whole has resulted from a development *away from* the original *Meistersprache* writing from which the Japanese syllabary component is absent. Such writing examples also illustrate the need to distinguish historical periods of *Sprachbund* pattern, in some cases marked off by sudden breaks in writing system used while other features are developing more gradually.

4.4.3 *Sprachbund* (Becker) and linguistic relativity

Betz, (referred to by Öhman, quoted by Lyons 1963: 42–3), talks of an 'abendländische Begriffsgemeinschaft', coinciding (Lyons comments) with Whorf's idea of Standard Average European. Öhman goes on to say that we can similarly in the Far East demarcate a linguistic community (or at least to Lyons it is linguistic) uniting Buddhist societies.

According to Ellis (1966e; 107) there may be some doubt whether languages of Buddhist communities do form a *Sprachbund* parallel to the countries that constituted medieval European Christendom. While religion, not to say ideology generally, is clearly a primary factor in the formation of many *Sprachbünde* (and is even reflected in choice of writing medium (4.4.2) without basic *Sprachbund* difference, as in the case of Serbo-Croat (the two major versions of the (Greco-)Romano-Cyrillic Alphabet here encoding one identical system), it is not the only factor, and religion-discontinuities do not always correspond to *Sprachbund* ones. There are and were forms of Christianity outside the European *Sprachbund*.

If there are in any sense Sanskrit-based and Pali-based *Bünde* in the communities of the Greater (Northern) and Lesser (Southern) Vehicles of Buddhism, they may be expected to concern only Buddhist terminology and phraseology, and the first to be weaker, because that branch of Buddhism is less unitary, and quite unlike the Sanskrit *Sprachbund* within India. Historically, partial Indo-Chinese membership of the Chinese *Sprachbund* (associated with the vicissitudes of writing systems) might be stronger than any Buddhist *Bund*.

Rather than simply between religion and *Sprachbund*, we may well see a general correlation between militancy of a religion and strength of *Sprachbund*.

4.5 BALKAN-TYPE *SPRACHBÜNDE*

4.5.1 *Sprachbund* (pre-Becker) and language functions

Unlike the minimum qualification for constituting a *Sprachbund* in Becker's sense, which goes only so far as very extensive borrowing of individual items, mostly lexical, and apparent convergence in patterns of lexis and phraseology (cp. n.2), the essential qualifications for constituting a *Sprachbund* 'in the pre-Becker sense' (other than a simply phonological one) include convergence in some grammatical categories (on the exponence relations involved in this and in language-genetic relationship see Ellis 1967: final section), and these may belong to any of the components of the grammar corresponding to the language-functions listed in 4.2.1.

Examples of the experiential include, in the convergence area formed by the westernmost languages of Europe (Lewy 1942 and 1952), the Romance (Spanish, Portuguese, also Italian) use of Latin stare for contingent being (Ellis 1971b) parallel to Irish tá. For examples of 'be' in Balkan see 4.5.3.

Examples of the logical, in Halliday's sense (1977: §§1.1-2, 4.4, 5.1.A) of grammatical systems characterized by recursion (in unit-complexes), include the 'serial verb' structures of many African languages. One use of these corresponds to use of prepositions in English and other languages, and may underlie the pidgin and creole treatment of prepositions discussed in 4.6.2 (Ellis 1971a, forthcoming c).

Examples of the interpersonal include, in the Balkan languages Turkish and Bulgarian, and to some extent Macedonian, the 're-narrative' system of the verb distinguishing possible relations of the speaker to the verifiability or attitudes to the truth of the experiential meaning (Ellis 1952, 1966a: 29, 1966d: 131) and partly corresponding to uses of the English logical-component system of indirect speech.

Examples of the textual include, in Balkan languages, the pattern of uses of the definite article (Ellis 1967: index of correspondence (in a small textual sample) higher between Greek, Rumanian and Bulgarian than between them and other languages sampled). The Albanian use of the anticipatory pronoun object when the definite article etc. is anaphoric contrasting with standard Macedonian undifferentiated use (Ellis 1966d: 131) exemplifies difference of extent of convergence with a convergence area.

4.5.2 *Sprachbund* (pre-Becker) and culture contact

The cultural background of Balkan convergence has been mentioned above (4.2.3). Its importance, and controversial aspects, as a paradigm case of *Sprachbund* in the narrower sense, lies in where we are to place on the cline (Ellis 1967) between Bloomfield's 'cultural' (cp. 4.2.2) and 'intimate' the nature of the historical contacts postulated ranging from Greek higher-cultural domination (Sandfeld's general explanation) to mobility of shepherds across linguistic frontiers. What seems certain is that no one extra-linguistic relation between the communities concerned explains all the linguistic relations between Balkan languages, and a complex of disparate linguistic features has to be confronted with one of both intimate and less intimate extra-linguistic contacts, within which identification of individual causal connections is of varying feasibility. And the full extent of the common linguistic features, as Seidel asserts, has not yet been plumbed.

4.5.3 *Sprachbund* (pre-Becker) and linguistic relativity

Most of the Balkan languages being Indo-European, differentiated verbs of 'being' (4.6.3) play little part in Balkan convergence.

The distinction that Turkish makes within 'being' of existence or presence (English there is, etc.), by var, negative yok, Bulgarian makes by ima, 'has', negative njama, with object, parallel to French il y a, Chinese you, etc. (e.g. njama go, 'he isn't present', Cameroon Pidgin (4.6.3) i now dey).

In colloquial Turkish, the 'be' form -dir, with any kind of complement, has interpersonal uses of the kind mentioned in 4.6.3, renarrative system, and, in Turkish generally, in the renarrative system of all verbs the presence or absence of this element (-dir/tir) in the 'non-witnessed' or reporting (it is said that . . .) form (-miş(-)), in all persons, makes a further distinction between belief and uncommittedness. In Bulgarian this use of the corresponding e, 'is', sa, 'are', is confined to the third person of this form.

These facts in themselves are sufficiently explained by the grammatical constraints (on the exponential resources for calquing) of the language-types involved (Ellis 1952, 1967) without recourse to considerations of linguistic relativity, but need to be put beside the evidence in 4.6.3 for and against 'being' as a case of linguistic relativity.

4.5.4 *Sprachbund* (pre-Becker) and interlanguage etc.

As Ellis (1967) points out, one application of Balkan comparative descriptive linguistics could be the devising of an information retrieval method for the languages on the basis of an 'interlanguage'[15] needing fewer additions for each language than between languages not within one *Sprachbund* of this kind. (The extent of this in detail may depend on the unplumbed more delicate extent of Balkan linguistic community (Seidel) referred to in 4.5.2.)

A quite different application of the same principle, in educational policy, is pointed out by Halliday, referring to Abdulaziz (1971: 160-1), who argues in effect that some of the minority languages of Tanzania are largely merely encodings in different exponents of the same formal or semantic systems as Swahili and therefore Swahili presents little difficulty as a medium of instruction for speakers of these languages—this is undoubtedly true of Swahili as compared with English. Cp. on the somewhat different situation in Ghana and other countries Ure 1972, also concerned with the applied semiotics of language-neutral visual materials (which would not necessarily be culture-neutral—or 'regional-'interlanguage' '-neutral').

4.6 PIDGINS AND CREOLES

4.6.1 Pidgins and Creoles and *Sprachbünde*

Pidgins and creoles relate to *Sprachbünde* in various ways. It is evident that they lie on the peripheries of *Sprachbünde*, and Becker considers pidgins most likely where one *Sprachbund* meets another. (53, 'Randerscheinung . . . , die namentlich dort vorzukommen scheint, wo sich zwei Sprachbünde begegnen.') More particularly, Weinreich (1958) argues that the creoles of the Caribbean form a *Sprachbund* (in some sense) of the 'upper languages', i.e. the convergence between upper language and original native language(s) embodied in the creole makes the upper language at the same time convergent with other upper languages. Furthermore, the idea of successive pidgins or creoles with different upper languages as 'relexifications' of one basic grammar (originating according to this hypothesis in the earliest Portuguese pidgin) makes them a *Sprachbund* (Balkan-type) in themselves, with the 'interlanguage' properties of a *Sprachbund* treated in 4.5.4.

In exemplifying West African and Pacific (English) pidgins, and indeed pidgins and creoles generally, I use Cameroon Pidgin English and Neo-Melanesian because:

a. each is the most highly institutionalized (in a sense standardized[16]) of its type and with the most creolization (G. Sankoff has recently brought detailed textual evidence (cf. 4.6.2) of Melanesian Tok Pisin as mother-tongue in community use, with reinforcing peer-group use in children of tribally mixed marriages).
b. among West African pidgins and creoles, including the creole Krio of Sierra Leone, Cameroon is pure West African in a sense that Krio is not, to some extent, though the extent to which Krio is in origin creole, or pidgin, brought back to West Africa from the Americas is currently a matter of dispute.

4.6.2 Pidgins and creoles and language functions

The ways in which pidgins or creoles differ from their base-languages
(upper languages) include grammatical categories belonging to all the
functional components listed in 4.2.1.

An example of experiential is the treatment of prepositions (i.e.
(formally) the place of prepositions in the system or (semantically)
the expression of what in English is expressed by prepositions, cp.
4.5.1). Neo-Melanesian has two principal prepositions, **long** (at, to,
from, etc.) and **bilong** ('of', '-'s', Cameroon Pidgin usually preposed
possessive like **got i buk**, 'God's book'); Cameroon Pidgin has more
simple prepositions (e.g. **witi, afta, bifo**) but one principal one, **fo**
(Schneider's (1966: 152) statistics of correspondence, p. 152: in
76, to 39, for 25, on 24, of 23, at 21, into 10, by 8, from 8, with 4,
during 1). The distinctions made by the many prepositions of English
are made in Neo-Melanesian (NM), and to some extent Cameroon
Pidgin (CP), by the addition of adverbs, which may be regarded as
forming a compound preposition, e.g. NM **namel long wit**, 'in the
midst of the wheat' (Matthew 13:25), CP **fo (-) insai drai kontri**,
'into the wilderness' (Mark 1:12), or local nouns, e.g. CP **fo yu bifo**,
'ahead of you' (Mark 1:2), where the low tone of **yu** (as marked by
Schneider 1966: 147) indicates that it is possessive to **bifo**, or by
the choice of verb, in the context, with the generalized preposition,
e.g. NM **kamap long graun**, 'is of the earth' ('comes from', beside
kam or **kamap** or **go long**, 'come to', and cp. John 4:7 **i kam bilong
pulimapim wara**, 'came to draw water') (John 3:31, given at more
length below under relative clauses, with **bilong dispela graun** complement to zero 'be' (4.6.3), cp. French (etc.) **je l'ai pris/enlevé** etc.
à mon frère, 'I took it from my brother'), or by a combination of
verbs (as in 4.5.1). Cp. Voorhoeve 1962 quoted in Ellis 1971a with
contrasting reference to Brøndal's ethnocentrism.

An example of logical is relative clauses. In NM until recently
a relative clause was, at least when written, indistinguishable in its internal constituency from a free clause with pronoun or zero subject or
other clause element, e.g. (with zero subject in the relative clause **i
kamap long graun** and resumptive pronoun **em** after it) **man i kamap
long graun, em i bilong dispela graun**, 'he that is of the earth is earthly'
(John 3:31). Curiously enough (contrasting with development of prose
resources in traditional languages, cp. Hill 1958: 448), an elaboration
(explicit marking off) of this seems not to be coming first in written
registers (developed till recently by missionaries etc.) but in the spoken
language of communities with mother-tongue speakers (4.6.1 above),
reported by Sankoff 1975a (with copious textual examples) and

Sankoff 1975b (cp. also Wurm and Mühlhäusler 1982: 82): the adding of ia (in origin demonstrative adverb ('here', 'there', English here) used as determiner like Welsh (y . . .) yma/yna or French (ce . . .)-ci/là) at the beginning and/or end of the clause (cp. Akan article no after relative clause, Ellis 1971c). In CP the structure is more like English with explicit relative pronoun e.g. som man, we i krai fo drai kontri, 'one crying in the wilderness' (Mark 1:3), but cp. got i buk, we got tok sey, 'God's book, where God says (that)' (Mark 1:2).

An example of interpersonal is the greater differentiation of first and/or second person pronouns. Both NM and CP distinguish singular and plural in the second person (as English does only in the reflexive yourself, yourselves), NM yu, yupela (also dual yutupela, trial yutripela), CP yu, wuna. NM distinguishes inclusive 1st + 2nd person, yumi, and exclusive 1st (+ 3rd) person (French nous autres), mipela (mitupela, mitripela), in CP both wi.

An example of textual, and of 'being' (cp. 4.6.3, mainly experiential), is CP na (4.6.3) with marked theme (exemplified in 4.6.3), a structure similar enough to the English it's . . . that . . . in relation between function and form but differing in detail of the latter both syntagmatically and systematically.

4.6.3 Pidgins and creoles and linguistic relativity

Verbs of 'being' have acquired prominence in discussion of 'linguistic relativity' e.g. Verhaar (1967 onwards), and other references in Ellis 1971b. Pidgins and creoles are not included in the languages in Ellis 1971b, but the pidgin treatment of English 'to be', exemplified in Figure 4.3 below, illustrates two things:

1. It constitutes some of the interlingual linguistic data on which to base a judgement on this language-philosophical example of the general Whorfian problem (cp. Ellis 1963b): whether different expressions, involving different segmentation, at word-rank as distinct from clause-rank, of the semantic field of 'being' in different languages, have caused, to any extent, differences in the philosophies (I mean scholarly philosophy) of different cultures, and more generally differences in the world-view of the ordinary individual. The latter, and the former in its relation to the latter, would require also psycholinguistic investigation (on difficulties in which cp. Ellis and Boadi 1969: 64-5, but whatever the practical feasibilities the theoretical interest remains as a problem in general vis-à-vis linguistic semiotics).

2. It also illustrates the way in which pidgins (and creoles, the creoles of the Atlantic seaboard being partly similar to West African pidgins in this) take the linguistic resources of English and rearrange them into a different realization relation with the semantics, thereby suggesting possible evidence for (1) above, about the semantics itself (asserting itself against the grain of the original English.

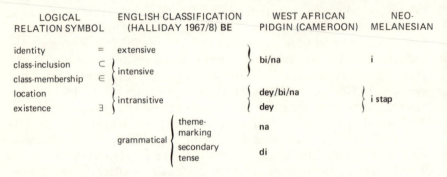

LOGICAL RELATION SYMBOL		ENGLISH CLASSIFICATION (HALLIDAY 1967/8) BE		WEST AFRICAN PIDGIN (CAMEROON)	NEO-MELANESIAN
identity	=	extensive			
class-inclusion	⊂	intensive		bi/na	i
class-membership	∈				
location		intransitive		dey/bi/na	i stap
existence	∃			dey	
		grammatical	theme-marking	na	
			secondary tense	di	

Figure 4.3 'To be' in two pidgins.

NM simply gets rid of the English item **be** (which survives only, in some Pacific pidgins, in the participial form in the tense-marker **bin**), and replaces it in one set of uses by the item derived from English **stop**.

CP continues to use the **be** item, **CP bi**, for all English uses except existing without a specified location or 'there is', but at the same time introduces alternative items: **dey** (from English **there**) for location, e.g. **got bi/dey fo heben**, 'God is in heaven', or (Schneider 1966: 81) **masa fan-boi i dey dey**, 'Mr Fineboy is in' ('present', cp. 4.5.1) beside (ibid.: 118 and 182) **i bin bi fo som bik sitik**, 'was in a big tree', and the sole item for bare existence, e.g. **got dey**; and **na** preceding marked thematic subject or complement of and replacing verb of any non-existential kind of 'be'-clause or marking theme of other clauses, or non-initially in the whole clause taking the place of 'be' verb or following **bi** before complement thereby marked as 'new' (cp. n.3), e.g. **na dina**, 'it's a feast' (Schneider 1966: 118, 189), **na got fo heben** or **na got dey/bi fo heben**, 'it is God that is in heaven', **na got dey**, 'it is God that exists', **na gon ansa i**, 'he was greeted by a gun' (ibid.: 102, 162), **na dai dis/dis, na dai**, 'this is death' (ibid. 80, 187), **josef, na kapenta**, 'Joseph is a carpenter' (ibid.: 81), **dis man'go dem bi na shwit wan**, 'these mangoes are sweet ones' (ibid.: 133).

I said above, in briefly indicating the case for pidgin data as evidence *for* a Whorfian answer to the 'being' question, that the semantics (i.e. of the 'x' languages) in x Pidgin y (y = English), to use Hall's formula, 1966) 'asserts itself against the grain of the original English'; but the alternative view is that essentially the Pidgin systems and realizations are following, and bringing out, the grain of the deeper grammar of the English, as described by the classes of clause and verb of Halliday 1967/8. Another example of this kind of relation between English and Pidgin is the CP **di** (presumably in origin a variant of **dey**, since Atlantic creoles (as well as coastal West Cameroon and Nigerian **dey** (Schneider 1966: 70)) have one form (e.g. Sranan Tongo **de**, Krio **de**) in both uses, e.g. Sranan Tongo, John 3:31 (cp. 4.6.2) 'Ma disoema komopo na grontapo, hem de vo grontapo en a de taki grontapo tori.') carrying on the function of English grammatical **be** in combination with the **-ing** (CP zero) form of the verb, Halliday's logical component category secondary tense, but not recursive with the other tense-system-terms in the same way in CP (cp. Ellis 1966b: 88–9).

For a non-pidgin example of the grammar of non-unitary 'be' asserting itself in language contact see 4.2.1.

4.6.4 Pidgins and creoles and register networks

The register pattern in the development between unilingualism and bilingualism in the process of creolization of pidgins (cp. n.16) may be stated in terms of compound and co-ordinate bilingualism (some references on this application of these terms: Ellis forthcoming a §3.21) thus: a pidgin begins as a co-ordinate partner in bilingualism with either of the two original languages involved, then may become for the speakers of the indigenous language a vehicle of some new registers (especially if now an 'in-pidgin', n.16), hence a compound partner. When it then reaches the point of being a creole, there is unilingualism, but a new bilingualism, or bidialectism (in-diglossia), with the upper language (or, bilingualism, with another 'upper' language, as in Surinam, English creoles with Dutch), may arise, again at first compound with the upper language providing further new registers. If there is further development to a 'post-creole' situation (Ellis forthcoming a §3.15), this is characterizable as unilingualism with marked (post-diglossic) variety-difference among (in a complex way) sets of registers.

Data for possible networks or other schematizations of the social varieties with possible register uses on the cline between ·'pure' pidgin (near creolization, n.16) and upper-language local varieties would include such text as the versions ('assimilated' (to indigenous languages)—'broad'—'anglicized') of the same CP text (Schneider 1966: 218-19) with some account of the sociolinguistic situation ibid.: 9-11).

It would be more difficult to parallel the networks referred to in 4.3.3, from the pidgin component of 'post-pidgin' trilingual situations (Ellis, forthcoming a §3.222-3), such as the Ghanaian, where the pidgin, though an 'in-pidgin' (namely West African Pidgin) in the sense of n.16, is exclusively unwritten, the principal uses of contemporary CP being, in the Ghanaian 'post-pidgin' situation, assumed by varieties of English itself or new registers of indigenous languages.

4.7 CONCLUSION

Many other examples could be given, both more examples of the matrix cells already exemplified and examples of some of the other cells in Figure 4.1. But the examples above will perhaps suffice to demonstrate some of the complexities of the possible relations between the study of languages in contact and the investigation of the place of language in social semiotic and culture generally.

NOTES

1. Though this postulated branch is not as unitary, or uncontroversial in its postulation, as the Votaic branch to which Northern Ghanaian languages belong.
2. Cp. Lyons 1963: 42-3, quoting Öhman, on European (Lyons says 'Western European') 'cultural overlap' in linguistic expression (including also the semantic distinctions themselves), Hill 1958: 447, identifying Becker's *Meistersprachen* (see below, c. in general) as koines of 'former cultures', and distinguishing between borrowed 'phonological form' and 'loan-translation' (cp. n.6), and Becker 1948: 36ff. and 85, where he distinguishes six stages of loan(-translation) -**Wanderung**, exemplified by stage 1 Romance **impression** to stage 6 Finnish **vaikutus** —we may compare Chinese yìnxiàng, 'stamp + image' or gănxiăng, 'feel + think'.

    Another example of an everyday word is **battle**, French **bataille** (from (**se**) **battre**), Italian **battaglia**, etc., German **Schlacht** (from **schlagen**), Russian **bitva** (from **bit'(sja)**), as compared with Chinese zhàndòu, 'war + fight', **huìzhàn**, 'meet + war' or **jiāozhàn**, 'join + war'.

    Such examples could be multiplied almost endlessly, though this generalization needs qualifying in certain ways (as Becker recognizes in his own terms in his discussion referred to above).

    Firstly, no one to my knowledge has even attempted statistics (within delimited semantic fields or other kinds of sample) of such examples and counter-examples.

Secondly, some examples are conditioned by the fact that European languages belong together in morphological typology—and this antedates the Greco-Roman *Sprachbund*. For example, Chinese has nothing corresponding to the **-le/-aille/-t/-tya** in the 'battle' words that could have been used in the Chinese word.

Thirdly, within each European language, especially perhaps ones that have shown as much resistance to 'foreign influence' as German or (Hill 1958: 447) Icelandic, there is variety of correspondence.

An example of both the second and third points is provided by a term like the Chinese **tónghuà**, 'assimilation': 'same +change', beside **assimilation**, Russian **upodoblenie** (from **podobnyj**), German **Angleichung** (from **gleich**), **Anpassung**, etc., where the **huà** which may be said to correspond to **ad-** (+ **-ation**), German **an-** (+ **-ung/-en**), (**tóng** certainly corresponding to **-simil-**, German **gleich**) is necessarily more specific, other lexemes being used in other words corresponding to **ad-** (+ **-tion**) ones, e.g. **jiāshēn**, 'increase + deep', **biànhuài**, 'change + spoil' beside **èhuà**, 'bad + change', 'aggravation', and the element in German **verähnlichen** to which it corresponds is the prefix **ver-** but in German **Umwandlung** partly the lexeme **-wandel-**.

A full account of the matter would need to correlate the semantic patterns and morphological resources of all the alleged *Meistersprachen*, and other members of *Sprachbünde*, of various periods (allowing for Reifler's 'semantic universals'). However, it is clear enough on general grounds of indelicate-linguistic and extra-linguistic evidence that such historical relations of borrowing and calquing (n.6) do exist between languages with cultural affinities (on which cp. n.5).

3. For information structure, theme, etc. see Halliday 1967/8, 1970, Ellis and Boadi 1969, Ellis 1978.

4. Usually one verb of being, that expressing (possibly *inter alia*) identity (e.g. the Irish **is** quoted), is used in the textual function referred to. In Akan, however, where the verb of identity **ne** is necessarily textually marked (Ellis 1971b, 1978), the verb that expresses attribution (class-membership/ inclusion) **yɛ** is also used, especially in the negative, person inanimate **ɛyɛ**, 'it is (was), in the third, negative **ɛnyɛ** (Ellis and Boadi 1969, Ellis 1971b), e.g. **mene no**, 'I am he', **ɛnhɛ ono ne hann no**, 'He was not that light', (**ɛyɛ**) **ɔbarima no na ɔbaa ha**, 'it was the man that came here', negative **ɛnyɛ, barima . . .**, 'it wasn't the man . . .'.

5. The kinds of culture involved in the cultural affinities referred to in n.2 accumulate through history till they range from the international science and technology (cp. n.8) of the latest 'new lexicon', Greco-Latin in Europe, to the 'intimate' vocabulary that was 'new lexicon' in the earliest times.

6. Cp. n.2 on calque/loan-translation. On calqued phraseology see Becker 1948: 83: 'Auge um Auge', 'Man kann nie wissen' (with variations), etc., 'in ganz Europa'.

7. For an elementary treatment, Corder 1973: 68–72.

8. The diagram shows the *main* cultural uses of each kind of language used in Ghana. As regards the language–culture connections excluded in the diagram:

(a) use in a tribal culture of a language other than the mother-tongue: traditionally, only that of another Ghanaian language for certain rituals, e.g. Akan by Gãs; any extensive use of another language would mark the disintegration of the given tribal culture itself, as well as the mother-tongue, e.g. the encroachment on 'Togo remnant languages' of Ewe language and culture.

(b) use in Ghanaian urban (inter-tribal, national) culture of non-Ghanaian English: this is as real (though less in extent) as that in 'international culture' in Ghana, in so far as e.g. laws are or have been drafted by users of non-Ghanaian English, but of course the linguistic differences in these registers between native and second-language English are slight.

(c) use in 'international culture' of a Ghanaian language: this is the principal change in use-distribution of the languages of Ghana now possible, with the recent official reintroduction of use of Ghanaian languages as one medium of instruction in primary schools.

9. It may be that the various, and socially varied, francophone West African societies use passenger lorries less. A francophone study, from a grammatical point of view, of a distant parallel, bar-signs, is Renaud 1971.

10. Strictly, developing languages of developing countries. Hindi–Urdu, for example, is a language of a developing country but already a developed language (or two, developed as Urdu and as Hindi, cp. 4.2.2), and (for example according to R. Hasan's testimony) mixture with English differs from the type here treated.

11. At least in the Ghanaian case, where linguistically the text-constituency indicates English within Ghanaian language, and sociolinguistically such observers as G. Ansre testify that the usual language of the registers in which mixed speech occurs is, if the participants have a Ghanaian language in common, a Ghanaian language rather than English.

12. Cp. 4.5.4 on possible alternative exponence of common categories or items.

13. Lyons 1968: 39 says 'Spoken Turkish did not change as a result of the replacement of the Arabic script by the Roman in 1926'. This is true in itself; but at the same time the writing reform was associated with a movement to turkicize the more obtrusive Arabic and Persian 'new lexicon' (n.5) and lexico-grammatical aspects of phraseology which has made contemporary literary Turkish, spoken and written, a different language-variety from the old Osmanli.

14. The complexity of the full Japanese script (used in the most usual written registers) could be defended on the general lines of Firth and others' apologia for the polysystemic orthography, within the alphabetic type, of English. It includes the use for the Chinese lexical element (as well as for native items) of the logographic-type component (characters), and within the syllabic writing-type component the use of the katakana syllabary for loans from other languages (as well as in italic- or capitals-equivalent uses), beside the hiragana syllabary for Sino-Japanese items not written with the characters (and the post-war orthographical reform reducing characters has increased the non-grammatical use of hiragana); this represents a (partial) correspondence between writing and *Sprachbund*-origin constituency of the language's present lexicogrammatical resources, admittedly now a more partial correspondence than that in English spelling between origin of items and Albrow's three 'systems' in the orthography, but with the graphic components themselves clear-cut as the English three 'systems' are far from being.

15. This essentially computational (i.e. computer-) use of the term *interlanguage* is not to be confused with that in the applied linguistics of language teaching,

e.g. Corder 1973, meaning learners' approximative systems, but there are clearly some theoretical links between them, an interlanguage in the second sense involving a very special case of relation between encodings and the encoded, of which interlanguage in the first sense (with no specific linguistic exponents) is a general case.

It should perhaps be noted, referring to the point in '4.2.2 in general' that Balkan languages belong to different Becker-*Sprachbünde* as regards 'new lexicon', that to the extent that information retrieval in practice is concerned with fields using much 'new lexicon' of the latest kind (n.5) the *lexical* advantage of such a lexicogrammatical information retrieval method might be found rather in application to a (live) Becker-type *Sprachbund*—though in fact the semantic distinctions in such contemporary terminology are largely identical between *Sprachbünde*.

16. On standard languages as the highest form of, or within, koines see Hill 1958, Ellis 1965a. A pidgin is by definition (as no one's mother-tongue) a koine, between upper language and indigenous language(s); NM and CP are eminently also koines between speakers of the different indigenous languages themselves, and the koine in this sense, between the local varieties of the pidgin, has already, before creolizing development has been completed, been to some extent standardized in the written use of missionaries, official agencies, etc.—and now, especially with Papua New Guinea political developments, standards are being set also in spoken NM, as W. Davenport testifies with anecdotes of language–attitudes (cp. Wurm and Mühlhäusler: 1982).

Discussion of such matters might be facilitated by the introduction of terms, say 'out-pidgin' and 'in-pidgin', distinguishing between pidgin in its origin in use between upper-language speakers and the local inhabitants (or transported slaves or labourers) and the pidgin developed into use (as a more conventional kind of koine) between speakers of the different local languages. (Cp. Todd 1974: 'restricted and extended pidgin'.) A pidgin can show some of the linguistic features, and of the sociolinguistic features of register-range, that may result from creolization, before there is institutional creolization in the usual sense of mother-tongue use, if it has become an in-pidgin; so that for some purposes in-pidgins (e.g. pre-creole NM) are to be classified with creoles rather than with out-pidgins. (A further terminological constraint in accepted usage is that while pidgins with both in-pidgin and out-pidgin uses are 'pidgins', creoles with both mother-tongue and non-mother-tongue (either 'in' or 'out') uses (e.g. Krio) are, in any use, 'creoles' —the latter use being distinguishable as 'creole koine'. Cp. Ellis forthcoming a: §3.222.)

Cp. also 5.4.

BIBLIOGRAPHY

Abdulaziz, M. H. (1971), 'Tanzania's national language policy and the rise of Swahili political culture', in W. H. Whiteley (1971: 160-78).
Bazell, C. E. *et al.* (1966) *In Memory of J. R. Firth*, London, Longman.
Becker, H. (1948), *Der Sprachbund*, Leipzig.
Bloomfield, L. (1933), *Language*, New York, Holt, Rinehart and Winston.
Brøndal, V. (1950), *La théorie des prépositions*, Copenhagen.

Corder, S. P. (1973), *Introducing Applied Linguistics*, London, Penguin.

Criper, L. (1971a), 'A classification of types of English in Ghana', *Journal of African Languages*, 10, Part 3, 6–17.

Criper, L. (1971b), 'The tone system of Ga English', in Houis, (ed.) (1971: 43–58).

Ellis, J. (1952), 'Contribution on affinité grammaticale', 7th International Congress of Linguists, London.

Ellis, J. (1963a), 'Possible comparisons of Balkan north-west European linguistic community, with reference to system-reduction method of quantification', *Slavjanska Filologija* (Bulgarian preprints for Fifth International Congress of Slavists), Sofia, Vol. 3: 291–9) (= 1966a, Appendix F: 142–53).

Ellis, J. (1963b), review of L. Jost, *Sprache als Werk und Wirkende Kraft . . .seit Wilhelm von Humbolt*, in *German Life and Letters*, 17.

Ellis, J. (1965a), 'Linguistic sociology and institutional linguistics', *Linguistics*, 19: 5–20.

Ellis, J. (1965b), review of Lewy (1942), *Journal of Linguistics*, 1: 203–4.

Ellis, J. (1966a), *Towards a General Comparative Linguistics*, The Hague, Mouton.

Ellis, J. (1966b), 'On contextual meaning', in Bazell (1966: 79–95).

Ellis, J. (1966c), 'On linguistic prehistory', in Ellis (1966a, Appendix E).

Ellis, J. (1966d), 'Rank-bound translation and areal convergence', in Ellis 1966a, Appendix D.

Ellis, J. (1966e), review of Lyons (1963), *Linguistics*, 24: 85–115.

Ellis, J. (1967), 'The place of Balkan linguistics in general linguistic theory', *Linguistique Balkanique*, 12: 37–44.

Ellis, J. (1971a), *Linguistics in a Multilingual Society*, inaugural lecture, 1970, Legon.

Ellis, J. (1971b), 'Some dimensions of being in John, Chapter 1 (a 'transfer' presentation of descriptive comparison)', *Journal of African Languages*, 10, Part 3, 18–33.

Ellis, J. (1971c), 'The definite article in translation between English and Twi', in Houis (ed.) (1971: 367–80).

Ellis, J. (1976), 'The role of the concept of text in the elaboration of linguistic data', *York Papers in Linguistics*, 6 (1976: 91–107).

Ellis, J. (1978), 'Identification and grammatical structure in Akan and Welsh', in Wurm and McCormack (eds) (1978: 297–306).

Ellis, J. (forthcoming a), *The Contrastive Analysis of Language Registers*, Tübingen, Narr.

Ellis, J. (forthcoming b), 'Logical and textual meaning', in Halliday, M. A. K. and Fawcett, R. (eds), *Papers in Systemic Linguistics*.

Ellis, J. (forthcoming c), 'Textual meaning in an Akan folk-tale and its translation'.

Ellis, J. and Boadi, L. (1969), ' "To Be" in Twi', in Verhaar (ed.) 1969: 1–71.

Fawcett, Robin P. (1980), *Cognitive Linguistics and Social Interaction: Towards an Integrated Model of a Systemic Functional Grammar and the Other Components of a Communicating Mind*, Heidelberg, Julius Groos and Exeter University.

Ferguson, C. (1971), *Language Structure and Language Use*, A. S. Dil (ed.) Stanford.

Field, J. (1960), *Search for Security, An Ethno-psychiatric Study of Rural Ghana*, London.

Fishman, J. (1964), 'Language maintenance and language shift', *Linguistics*, 9.

Georgiev, V. (1966), 'Résumés des communications', 1st Congress of Balkan and South-East European Studies, Sofia.

Hall, R. A. (1966), *Pidgin and Creole Languages*, New York.

Halliday, M. A. K. 1967/8, 'Notes on transitivity and theme in English', *Journal of Linguistics*, 3: 37-84, 199-244; 4: 179-215.

Halliday, M. A. K. (1970), 'Functional diversity in language', *Foundations of Language*, 6, 322-61.

Halliday, M. A. K. (1974), 'Language as social semiotic: towards a general socio-linguistic theory', *LACUS/ALCEU Forum*, 1 (1974: 17-46).

Halliday, M. A. K. (1977), 'Text as semantic choice in social contexts', in van Dijk and Petöfi (eds) (1977).

Halliday, M. A. K., and Fawcett, R. P. (eds) (forthcoming), *Current Papers in Systemic Linguistics*, London, Batsford.

Hill, T., (1958) 'Institutional Linguistics', *Orbis*, 7, 441-5.

Houis, M. (ed.) (1971), *Actes du huitième Congrès de la Société Linguistique de l'Afrique Occidentale, Abidjan, 1969*, Abidjan.

Kloss, H. (1967), 'Types of multilingual communities', in Lieberson, ed. (1967: 7-17).

Lewy, E. (1942, reprinted Tübingen, Niemeyer, 1964), *Der Bau der europäischen Sprachen*, Proceedings of the Royal Irish Academy, 48.C.2, Dublin.

Lewy, E. (1952), contribution to the section 'Affinité grammaticale', Seventh International Congress of Linguists, London.

Lieberson, S. (ed). (1967). Explorations in Sociolinguistics, *International Journal of American Linguistics*, 33: 4, part = (1966) *Sociological Inquiry*, 36:2.

Lyons, J. (1963), *Structural Semantics*, Oxford, Blackwell.

Lyons, J. (1968), *Introduction to Theoretical Linguistics*, Cambridge, Cambridge University Press.

Perren, G. E. and Trim, J. (eds) (1971), *Applications of Linguistics*, Cambridge, Cambridge University Press.

Renaud, P., (1971), 'La phrase nominale a la porte des bars de Yaoundé', in Houis (ed.) (1971): 599-606).

Sandfeld, K. (1930), *La linguistique balkanique*, Paris, Champion.

Sankoff, G. (1975a), 'Data and interpretation in sociolinguistics: syntax and discourse in New Guinea Tok Pisin', Linguistics Association York symposium on the nature of data in linguistics.

Sankoff, G., (1975b), 'Sampela nupela lo i kamap long Tok Pisin', K. A. McElhanon (ed.), *Tok Pisin i Go We?*, Port Moresby: 235-40.

Schneider, G. (1966), *West African Pidgin English*, Athens, Ohio.

Todd, L., (1974), *Pidgins and Creoles*, London, Routledge & Kegan Paul.

Ure, J. N. (1963), 'Metaphor in Balkan ballads', Fifth International Congress of Slavists, Sofia.

Ure, J. N. (1969), 'Practical registers', *English Language Teaching*, 23, 107-14, 206-15.

Ure, J. N. (1970), 'English in a multilingual community', Ninth West African Languages Congress, Freetown.

Ure, J. N. (1971), 'Lexical density and register differentiation', in Perren and Trim (eds) (1971: 443-52).

Ure, J. N. (1972), 'Mother tongue education and minority languages: A question of values and costs', International Consultation on Language Planning, Legon, (revised 1981) *Journal of Multilingual and Multicultural Development*, 2: 303-8.

Ure, J. N., (1974), 'Code-switching and "mixed speech" in the register systems of developing languages', *Proceedings of the Third International Congress of AILA, Copenhagen, 1972*, Heidelberg, Julius Groos, 222-39.

Ure, J. N., (1975), 'Register systems of a language in L1 and L2 communities', Fourth International Congress of AILA. Stuttgart; supplementary report of The Language Diary Project (The Range of Language Use among Primary School Teachers: SSRC Project, HR 2268/1).

van Dijk, T. and Petöfi, J., (eds) (1977), *Grammars and Descriptions*, Berlin, de Gruyter.

Verhaar, J. W. M., (ed.) (1967 onwards), *The Verb 'Be' and its Synonyms*, Dordrecht, Reidel.

Voorhoeve, J. (1962), 'Creole languages and communication', *Symposium on Multilingualism*, Brazzaville.

Weinreich, U. (1953), *Languages in Contact*, New York, LCNY.

Weinreich, U. (1958), 'On the compatibility of genetic relationship and convergent development', *Word*, 14, 374-9.

Whiteley, W. H., ed (1971), *Language Use and Social Change*, London, Oxford University Press.

Wurm, S. and McCormack, W. (eds) (1978), *Approaches to Language*, The Hague, Mouton.

Wurm, S. and P. Mühlhäusler (1982), 'Registers in New Guinea Pidgin' in Ellis and Ure (eds), *Register Range and Change, International Journal of the Sociology of Language*, 35, 69-86.

5 Ways of saying: ways of meaning

Ruqaiya Hasan

MacQuarie University, Sydney, Australia

5.1 CULTURE AND SEMIOTIC STYLES

5.1.1 Introductory remarks

Genuine dichotomies are probably rare; upon closer examination most turn out to be the by-product of some particular point of view.[1] For example, take the persistent dichotomy between the how and the what, the manner and the matter, the style and the content. When we say that **John can't swim** and its elliptical parallel **John can't** are two ways of saying the same thing, we subscribe to just such a dichotomy. The acceptance of such a view implies that meanings are immanent, with an existence independent of the expressive symbolic system, and that some kinds of meaning are matter whereas others are not. These beliefs are clearly the by-product of a particular view of human language; the opposite view underlies the belief that all kinds of meaning are matter, and that far from being immanent, meanings are the function of the relations that hold between the symbols of an expressive system. This polarization between the views is deliberate; I do not believe that the choice of one as against the other is determined by reality being thus and thus, but rather because a particular descriptive schema appeals to us as a convincing model of reality.

Having made this effort at impartiality, I wish to align myself quite definitely with the second view, in which the dichotomy between form and meaning is rejected. The text for this paper can be summed up in one sentence: different ways of saying are different ways of meaning—obviously not the same thing. How we say is indicative of how we mean. And a culture develops characteristic ways of meaning. These ways of meaning, in their totality, are specific to that culture; they constitute its *semiotic style*.

5.1.2 Semiotic and semantic styles

The term *semiotic style* covers not only characteristic ways of saying but also of being and behaving. I assume that these, taken together, exhaust the means by which men can mean. To say that there is a culture-specific semiotic style is to say that there is a congruence, a parallelism between verbal and non-verbal behaviour, both of which are informed by the same set of beliefs, values and attitudes.

The assertion that specific cultures have specific semiotic styles is neither totally evident nor incontrovertible. However, if examination reveals that ways of saying, being and behaving do run largely parallel to each other in a community, then the claim is plausible that there exist some organizing principles which have the effect of producing this congruence, this parallelism. The presence of the principles is productive of a unique set of attributes which characterizes all aspects of human behaviour in the community. It is this unique set of attributes found in the ways of being, behaving and saying that defines the character of a community's semiotic style. I would suggest that the very organizing concepts which control the congruence of the semiotic style are also the ones which underly that community's world view—and there is a good reason for the suggestion.

It is widely accepted that the universe is not entirely given: man has had to make sense of it—and in doing so, he may be said to have created it—at least in part. This universe is as much a construct of man's imagination, as it is a brute, concrete reality outside of him. Here, too, there are potential irreconcilables which must be allowed co-existence without creating permanent chaos. The congruence of the semiotic style can be said to arise out of the need to construct a design for the living of human life so that aspects of it do not militate constantly against each other. Thus to understand the basis of this congruence in a particular culture is tantamount to understanding that culture, even if only partially.

Logically the notion of semiotic style subsumes that of *semantic style*; the latter can be succinctly described as the style of meaning verbally. A characteristic semantic style prevalent in a culture must logically be in keeping with that culture's prevalent semiotic style.

5.1.3 Culture consonance and culture conflict

The definition of the boundaries of a culture is problematic. In the first place, there is the well-recognized fact that no culture is a homogeneous, monolithic system any more than any language is. Secondly, the idea of congruence applied to culture as a whole can be misleading if one is left with the impression that congruence is synonymous with 'total lack of conflict in ideology and/or practice'. There is quite obviously an intricate relationship between these two points, but a detailed discussion of neither can be undertaken in this paper.

It is, however, important to point out, first, that I believe the notion of culture to be variable in delicacy. Thus at a particular point in delicacy, we may be justified in maintaining that cultures (A) and (B) are distinct; this does not imply that at a point of greater delicacy we may not claim two distinct cultures (A1) and (A2) or (B1) and (B2). Equally, there may be environments in which the interest lies in a much more generalized comparison; if so, it would be valid to think of (A) and (B) as belonging to the same culture as opposed to (C) and (D). A recognition of the usefulness of shifting boundaries is found in such current terms, e.g. 'sub-culture' and 'culture-group'. It remains now to add that whatever is said here about 'culture' is applicable, *mutatis mutandis*, to 'sub-cultures'—and equally to distinguishable 'culture-groups'.

Turning to the question of conflict in culture, I do not believe that it could be thought of as a total rift or a complete divergence. The closest analogy that comes to mind in this respect is that of the linguistic relation of antonymy, which—as is well known—involves opposition between two terms. However, the assertion of opposition has significance only in an environment of a large degree of congruence. Thus the items **buy** and **sell** are opposites as are **long** and **short**, while it would be nonsense to make this claim with regard to **sell** and **throwaway** or **short** and **narrow**. It seems to me that conflict in culture—or between its sub-cultures—can be a meaningful concept only if the opposite of conflict, i.e. consonance or congruence, is also applicable to some other area(s) of the culture in focus.

Nor is there an insurmountable problem in relating the present view of semantic style with such a view of culture-with-conflict. Language is not a strait-jacket constraining its speakers into one invariable mould—indeed the notion of semantic style would be empty of significance in that case. The interest lies in the fact that while within the range of its systemic options each language provides a very wide set of resources for meaning, distinct sub-sets of its speakers characteristically select only a particular sub-set of the options permitted by the overall system. In comparing two languages we are thus concerned with two questions: one, how do the overall systems differ from each other; and secondly, what resources of the system are characteristically deployed by which section of the speakers. To talk about a characteristic semantic style is to imply the possibility of other semantic styles which are *not* characteristic. Style presupposes option; but the frequency of the selection of a particular set of options is itself a significant fact. It is this aspect that I particularly wish to explore in this paper.

5.1.4 Semantic distance

As cultures differ from each other in their characteristic semiotic styles, so do languages in their characteristic semantic styles. Fairly competent bilinguals often find themselves in a position so well-described by Wittgenstein (1921) as; 'we cannot find our feet with them'. This is not because the sounds and the wordings are unfamiliar but more because the ways of meaning are not familiar—the manner in which the universe is made meaningful is not fully apprehended.

Semantic distance across languages is created by the differences in characteristic ways of meaning. This distance across two languages cannot be measured by counting lexical gaps or by examining the difference in the relative referential domains of individual lexical items, e.g. cup or camel. Rather it would be far more profitable to study the basis for the organization of meanings—as I understand Whorf to have suggested—than to ask if two languages have an equal number of words for colours, camels, or snow—as Whorf is often reported to have said (Bolinger 1968; Brown 1970; Lenneberg 1971; Leech 1974). What is relevant to the exploration of the semantic distance between two languages is an account of the principles which govern and systematize their meanings. Asking whether the English physical eye perceives the same colour distinctions as the Hopi eye would be totally beside the point, as Whorf would have been the first to point out. The stone-ness of the stone and the cloud-ness of the cloud are both real and evident to human physical senses. However, this physical apprehension of the real and concrete does not bar the Indian from seeing the stone as divinity, or the Hopi from taking the cloud as animate. To me there seems to be no reason why the stone cannot be both that thing against which the toe may be stubbed painfully and that god which grants the wish of the heart. After all, 'seeing as' is no less real an experience than that of 'seeing'; and reality is neither stone nor god, but the concrete and the symbolic are definitely two major modes of reality. I certainly do not object to the fact that linguists pay attention to the unitary lexico-grammatical categories, or that they enquire into the literal referential relations; the point of my criticism is that they stop short of the goal, converting the means into the end of the enterprise and finishing with the atomistic examination which should have been no more than the bare start. Then, by some sleight of hand, the evidence regarding the concreteness of the stone is made to appear weightier and more decisive than the evidence regarding its symbolic status as divinity—as if what one should understand by the expression 'world view' is actual, physical viewing of concrete phenomena.

To develop the above themes, I shall examine two characteristic ways of saying; the *explicit* and the *implicit*, with particular emphasis on the latter. I shall try to show how a particular kind of implicit style is related to certain aspects of social structure, and how the latter affects the style of non-verbal behaviour, creating a congruence that extends over the entire semiotic domain. Using middle-class English and Urdu as comparable varieties of two distinct languages, I shall attempt to show how the semantic distance across these languages is in the last resort relatable to cultural differences between the two communities.

5.2 IMPLICIT AND EXPLICIT STYLES

5.2.1 Implicit and explicit ways of saying

The difference between explicit and implicit styles can be stated most conveniently in terms of what a normal person needs in order to interpret an utterance as it is intended by the speaker. Where explicit style is concerned, the correct interpretation of a message requires no more than a listener who has the average working knowledge of the language in question. When, however, the message is in the implicit style, its intended more precise meanings beome available only if certain additional conditions are met; the average working knowledge of the language is necessary but not sufficient. Consider for example:

1. Dill will.

The fact of simply knowing English does not equip one to provide the correct more precise interpretation of (1). This does not mean that the English speaker will fail totally to understand (1) or regard it as a non-sentence; however, what could be understood by (1) as it stands in isolation is something highly general, such as perhaps: **dill will be implicated in some process.** The precise nature of this process and the other participants and/or circumstances attendant upon it —if there are any—cannot be known, unless some clue is provided by a source that lies outside of (1). If, for example, we know that the full textual context for the occurrence of (1) is:

1a. Phlox
Won't grow on rocks.
Dill
Will.

we have no difficulty in arriving at the correct interpretation: **dill will grow on rocks**.

The two sentences of this 'poem' are examples of the two styles. While (1) exemplifies the implicit style of saying, the example below:

2. Phlox won't grow on rocks.

exemplifies the explicit style. The intended interpretation of (2) is available to a normal speaker without reference to any source of information extrinsic to the string itself. This, then, is the basic difference between the two styles: the explicit string is semantically self-sufficient; by contrast, the implicit string involves a semantic dependence. The precise meanings of the latter are not contained within itself but must be retrieved from some source extrinsic to the string.

5.2.2 Implicit devices

The distinction between implicit and explicit encoding is present most probably in all human languages. The construction of texts as we know them requires their presence side by side (Halliday and Hasan 1976; 1980; Hasan 1981). Still to refer to an entire string either as implicit or explicit could be inaccurate for the simple reason that it is seldom exclusively either the one or the other. Instead while some of the units in a string are implicit, others may be explicit. For example in (1), it is only the interpretation of the elliptical verbal group **will** that involves semantic dependence; the precise meaning of **dill** does not have to be retrieved from anywhere else any more than that of any of the units in (2).

From this point of view, implicitness in strings is variable, some being more implicit than others. The degree of implicitness, in this sense, is determined purely quantitatively, by comparing the proportion of the explicit units to the implicit ones. Compared with (1):

3. They will.

would be more implicit. In fact it is maximally so, since there is no unit in the string that is not implicit. The two ways of saying can be seen, then, as ranged upon a continuum, with the totally explicit and the totally implicit forming the two endpoints, each exemplified by (2) and (3) respectively, with (1) somewhere between the two.

An encoding unit which involves a semantic dependence for its precise interpretation will be referred to here as an *implicit device*. In the construction of texts such implicit devices play a major role because of the semantic links they establish with those segments by reference to which they may be interpreted. The implicit devices are, thus, a category of cohesive devices (Hasan 1981); however, the present paper is not concerned with the cohesive potential of these devices as such. The focus is largely upon how the interpretation of the implicit devices becomes available. For English these devices may be discussed under the familiar heading of *reference, substitution*, and *ellipsis* (Halliday and Hasan 1976; 1980; Hasan 1981).

5.2.3 The interpretation of implicit devices: endophora

Consider **dill will** again. The source of the interpretation of the elliptical verbal group **will** lies in the co-text, i.e. in a part of the accompanying text. When some part of the co-text forms the interpretative source for an implicit device, the interpretation is described as *endophoric*. **Will** in (1) is an implicit device, interpreted endophorically.

The interpretative source in the co-text may either precede the implicit device or follow it, as in (4) and (5), respectively:

4. Phlox won't grow on rocks. Dill will.

5. You won't believe it but they have accepted the entire scheme.

The interpretative source is underlined with broken lines; the implicit device itself with a solid line. When the source precedes the device, the interpretation is said to be *anaphoric*, as in (4) above. Where it follows the device, as in (5), the interpretation is said to be *cataphoric*.

5.2.4 The interpretation of implicit devices: exophora

The implicit device is not always textually interpreted; on occasions the source for its interpretation lies in the context, i.e. in the relevant situation in which the utterance is embedded. An example would be:

6. Don't!

called out to someone who is engaged in some activity that the speaker wishes to put an end to. When the interpretation depends upon the situationally provided clues, as it would in (6), then the interpretation may be said to be *exophoric*. **Don't** in (6) is an exophorically interpreted device; its intended precise meanings are situationally mediated.

In the following sections, I may refer to an implicit device as an anaphoric, a cataphoric, or an exophoric one. It is important, therefore, to state here quite clearly that the phoric status of the devices is not inherent; rather, it is determined from occurrence to occurrence of a device by reference to the location of the relevant interpretative source (Halliday and Hasan: 1976; 1980). In itself, the implicit device **don't** is neither endomorphic nor exophoric; its phoric status is variable. In (6) it is interpreted exophorically while in (7) the interpretation is endophoric:

7. -Do elephants like coca cola?

    -No, they don't.

5.3 ENDOPHORIC AND EXOPHORIC INTERPRETATION

5.3.1 Endophoric interpretation and implicit style

The endophoric device is interpreted by reference to some part of the co-text. Although co-text is variable in length, normal speakers have little or no difficulty in locating the interpretative source and in retrieving the intended meanings. This is because the intended meanings of the endophoric devices are not randomly sprinkled anywhere, anyhow in the text. The nature of the device itself often provides some specification of the nature of the interpretative source. This point can be demonstrated by a consideration of the implicit device **the**.

Speaking somewhat informally we may say that the function of **the** is to indicate definiteness for the (group of) thing(s) named by the noun that it modifies. But **the** is not the only device which renders its modified definite. What distinguishes **the** from other Modifiers is the fact that underlying it are only the following options: [SPECIFIC:NEUTRAL].

So while the presence of **the** indicates definiteness for the modified Thing, the item **the** itself has to be considered implicit because information regarding parameters relevant to definiteness are not built into the meaning of **the** itself. They must be retrieved from some other source. However, crucial properties of the interpretative source can be clearly stated, showing that the retrieval of the intended meanings is as much 'system-governed' as other productive patterns of the language.

When **the** is cataphoric, the interpretative source forms part of the same nominal group in which the cataphoric **the** occurs; and its structural function is normally that of Qualifier as in:

8. At dinner Mihrene sat opposite the old gentleman who was Papa's business friend.

The clause **who was Papa's business friend** functions as a Qualifier in the nominal group **the old . . . . . business friend**; the more specific intended meaning is located within the qualifier. The definiteness of the old man consisted in the fact that he was Papa's business friend. There are languages in the world, Urdu included, where this nominal group could be literally ordered as **Papa's business friend old gentleman.**

When **the** is anaphoric, a semantic link exists between the noun it modifies and the interpretative source which provides the parameter for definiteness. These semantic links may be those of synonymy or hyponymy or meronymy. Under synonymy, we may include reiteration and scatter as special cases. Each of these relations is exemplified below:

9. John's car was badly damaged. The rear left door was completely bashed in.
   [aforementioned car's rear left door; modified door is a meronym of car.]
10. He bought pearls, each one separately, each one perfect. He bought fragments of mother-of-pearl. He bought moonstones . . . . He bought jade and crystals and collected chips of diamonds . . . . . He kept the jewels first in a small cigarette box . . . .
    [aforementioned types of jewels; modified jewels is superordinate to pearls, mother-of-pearl, jade, crystal, and diamonds.]
11. The wind blew, the hat flew, hither and thither, in loops and hoops and landed at last on the bald head of Benito Bedaglio, a penniless veteran. "Don't shoot. I surrender", shouted the bewildered old soldier.
    [aforementioned veteran; modified soldier is synonymous to veteran.]
12. She was wearing last year's dress and choker of false pearls . . . . Ephraim saw the false pearls and suffered.
    [aforementioned pearls; modified pearls lexical reiteration.]
13. As you are aware, the Committee has recommended a cut-back in research funds. We are gathered here today to protest against the recommendation.
    [product of aforementioned act; modified recommendation related to recommend as lexical scatter.]

While the formal criteria for the recognition of the interpretative source from the co-text are clearly statable—as demonstrated above —there is no reason to suggest that the normal listener is aware of a search for such bits of the co-text. Subjectively the entire processing of meaning appears to be a simple act, performed painlessly in one single step. On hearing **Phlox won't grow on rocks. Dill will.**, the normal user of English knows how the elliptical verbal group **will** needs to be interpreted by the time he comes to the item; he is not conscious of engaging in a search for its precise meaning.

In understanding the complexity of the process of interpretation, the linguist must consciously analyse many meaning relations; it is such conscious analyses which form the basis of viable hypothesis about the location and nature of the interpretative source in the co-text. The linguist's findings have to be phrased in terms of the formal attributes of the implicit device and/or the interpretative source; but so far as the normal speaker is concerned, the operation is simply one of establishing correct relevances—that is, of being able to understand. This is demanding no more than that the speaker know his language; for knowing a language is, in Halliday's excellent phrase, only 'knowing how to mean' (Halliday 1975).

It follows from the above observations that so far as access to the more precise, intended meanings of the endophoric devices is concerned, there is no significant difference between the implicit devices and the explicit ones. While the correct interpretation of the explicit devices demands a working knowledge of the language, that of an endophoric device demands not only such knowledge but also the presence of the relevant part of the co-text. If both these conditions obtain, the normal speaker may not even be aware of the occurrence of such implicit devices. Not many of my readers will have taken a special note of **both these** and **such** in the previous sentence; but they will become aware of a qualitative difference between these items and others, e.g. **aware, occurrence**, if the sentence preceding the last one is not made available.

5.3.2 Exophoric interpretation and implicit style

It is not possible to make the same claims about the interpretation of the exophoric implicit devices. Here, the intended more precise meanings are mediated through the relevant extra-linguistic situation. This implies that the most natural environment for the use of exophoric devices is in face-to-face interaction, where the channel of discourse is spoken and visual contact between the speakers is present.

However, situation is a large word and covers different types of factors. If the interpretation of the exophoric device depends upon the situational factors, we need to be more precise about the specific nature of these factors. In the following discussion I shall suggest criteria for the sub-classification of the exophoric devices; these criteria themselves would be based upon the type of situational knowledge that is needed for the correct more precise interpretation of the exophorics.

First, we need to be more precise about the interactant relations. In the discussion of both the explicit and the endophoric devices, it was possible to operate with the neutral term 'listener'. I refer to this term as neutral because it makes no distinction between a causal hearer and the intended addressee. Both are assumed to be able to interpret equally successfully, which is, incidentally, a good indication of the fact that endophoric relations are as system-governed as the relations in the lexicon.

However, in discussing the interpretation of the exophorics, the first important distinction is that between the intended addressee and the casual hearer. The speaker *intends* the former to hear; the latter may just *happen* to overhear. The speaker's wording is fashioned for the former; the needs of the latter are in no way relevant to the interaction. Obviously, then, the speaker would assume that the more precise meanings of the exophoric devices are available to the intended addressee. This assumption is based on no more than the common sense observation that, in natural language use, one talks so that one's addressee can make sense of what one is saying (Firth 1950; Grice 1967). Nothing proves so cogently the fundamentally inter-organic nature of human language (Halliday 1975) as the frequency with which the speaker's expectation is fulfilled regarding his addressee's ability for correct interpretation.

The relatively peripheral status of the casual listener can be exploited in considering the interpretation of the exophorics. Since the speaker's wording is not fashioned with his needs in mind, he can be used as a test case. We may postulate that if a casual listener is able to interpret an exophoric correctly, then it is highly probable that such an exophoric would be correctly interpreted by the intended addressee as well. Thus in discussing the various types of exophorics the question I shall ask each time is: what does a casual listener need in order to be able to interpret this type of exophoric?

5.3.3 Instantial exophorics

Consider the following examples:

| 14a. Don't—— | [don't what?] |
| b. I'll need to get up a bit higher—— | [higher than what?] |

c. Do have some——   [some what?]

d. Which <u>one</u> would you like?   [which what?]

Let us assume that each example (14 a–d) represents a complete text; i.e. the possibility of endophoric interpretation does not exist. So, the question arises: how can we answer the queries in the left column?

If (14 a–d) are complete texts, then the implicit devices within them can only be interpreted by their relation to some aspect(s) of the material situational setting which also bears relevance to the text (Hasan 1981). The distinction implied between the material situational setting and the text-relevant context is necessary because the two are not synonymous. For example, the material situational setting surrounding the composition of this paper bears little or negligible relevance to the status of this paper as text. By contrast, for (14 a–d) we must assume a large degree of overlap between the material situational setting and the relevant context, which is another way of saying that aspects of the former constitute a part of the latter.

It follows then that a casual listener will be able to interpret the exophoric devices correctly so long as he has visual contact with the material situational setting. This is made all the easier for two reasons: first, the internal make-up of the message wherein the implicit devices occur provides a general indication of the essential nature of the relevant aspect of the material situational setting. For example, (14a) can only relate to a 'doing' of some sort; (14b) can only relate to three-dimensional objects that can serve as base for something or someone, while (14c–d) can only be said in relation to some concrete object. In other words the total semantic structure of the message provides a 'clue' as to where the listener's attention should be focused. In addition to this, the speaker's own body cues reinforce the listener's perception of the relevant bits of the material situation. So in order to arrive at a correct interpretation of (14 a–d), the casual listener should be able not only to overhear but also to see what is going on that engages the speaker and who or what else is implicated in these goings-on. Given this, the interpretation provided by the casual listener will be significantly close to that which the intended addressee will provide. However, the meaning of these same devices will become opaque to the casual listener, as soon as visual contact disappears. It can be concluded therefore that the precise meanings of the exophoric devices in (14 a–d) are mediated by relatively concrete 'bits' of the material situational setting, such as are amenable to perception.

I shall refer to this type of exophorics as *instantial exophorics*; an instantial exophoric is an implicit device whose precise meaning is mediated in a given instance only through some concrete elements of the goings-on surrounding the utterance in which the device occurs.

5.3.4 Intermediate exophoric

Superficially the following example appears to belong to the same type as (14 a–d):

15a. Don't touch the books.   [which books?]

but there are some interesting differences. If the casual listener is able to both hear and see, he will know what actual objects **the books** refers to in the material situational setting. However, being able to see the concrete entities does not necessarily imply that he will also know for certain what the the-ness of **the** in the nominal group **the books** consists of. This happens because of the nature of the definite article in English.

The simply indicates definiteness without actually providing any clue whatever about the nature of the parameters relevant to the definiteness. Clearly one source of definiteness can be the presence here-and-now of the entities to which the modified noun refers. Wherever the total semantic structure of the clause permits this interpretation, it can be employed as in the case of (15a). But it is not impossible that the speaker of (15a) has some parameter of definiteness in mind which goes beyond that of here-and-now. This might very well be the case in (15b):

15b. Don't touch the books. Mummy will be cross.

It seems highly plausible that in saying (15b) the speaker intends and is interpreted as saying **don't touch these-here-and-now books which in some way pertain to mummy (or she will be cross).** In this case, the intended precise meaning of **the** is not that of situational deixis only; it involves the relation of books to mummy.

And yet such an interpretation is not necessarily guaranteed by the presence of the second clause as a comparison of (15b) with the following will show:

15c. Don't play with the stones. Mummy will be cross.

Presumably the stones in question do not pertain to mummy; they are far more likely to be just these-here stones. And by the same token, it is just possible that **the books** in (15b) do not pertain to mummy—she may simply be against children touching books. There appears to be no way that we can be privy to such information except through knowing the life circumstances of the various protagonists involved. Thus there appears to be a genuine indeterminacy of intended meaning in the exophoric **the** of the type under consideration. The ability to see and hear does not necessarily guarantee the retrieval of all the intended meanings of the implicit device. Moreover, the casual listener has no means of finding out if he has understood all that there was to understand.

This genuine indeterminacy can be counter-balanced by certain other factors. Imagine that our casual listener is not able to see the goings-on for (14a–d) or (15a–c). Under this condition, he is likely to have a clearer idea of what is being talked about in (15a–c) than he would in (14a–d). This is for two reasons, and one of these has already been discussed above. The total semantic structure of the clauses in (15a–c) is such as to affirm the presence of books on the interactive scene. Thus the casual listener knows at least something about the books and stones being talked about. Note this is not simply because **the** occurs, but it is primarily because the semantics of the verb and the agreement between time of speaking and temporal reference within the clause permit such an interpretation. This can be indicated by a comparison of (15a–c) with the following:

15d. Go and fetch the man immediately.
15e. We played with the doll yesterday, didn't we?

The second reason for a clearer idea of what is being talked about in (15a–c) lies in the formal functioning of **the**. **The** is one of the very few Modifiers which cannot be 'pushed up' to function as Head in an elliptical nominal group (Halliday and Hasan 1976); it must be followed by some other nominal word(s). The degree to which the meanings of the nominal group with the exophoric **the** become available to the listener then depends partly on what follows **the**. If the exophoric **the** occurs in an elliptical group e.g. in:

15f. I'll have **the other** as well.
15g. I'll take **the bigger two**.

the access to meaning would be as restricted in the absence of visual contact as it would in (14a–d). If, on the other hand, the exophoric **the** occurs in a non-elliptical nominal group, the access to meaning is affected by the status of the modified noun. This can be seen from a comparison of the following:

16a. Look at the silly **thing**.

16b. Look at the silly **creature**.
16c. Look at the silly **fellow**.
16d. Look at the silly **boy**.

Here the four nouns are graded on the cline of specificity (see 5.4.3 below), with **thing** being the least specific and **boy** the most. If we assume that the situational referent of each one of these four items is the same entity, then the non-seeing casual listener knows most clearly what is being talked about in (16d), and least clearly in (16a). It is my impression that the characteristic environment for the occurrence of the exophoric **the** is as in (16d), i.e. in a non-elliptical nominal group where the modified noun has fairly high specificity. Thus in the light of the above discussion we find that although in (15a–c) there is a genuine indeterminacy in the precise meaning of **the**, it is also true that the casual listener is able to understand a good deal, though his understanding may be somewhat less complete than that of the intended addressee.

When an implicit device is genuinely indeterminate so that its intended precise meanings can vary in scope, so that the casual listener cannot be sure whether or not he has missed some significant information, then such an implicit device will be referred to as *indeterminate exophoric*. The only implicit device in English that is capable of being used in this manner is **the**.

5.3.5 Restricted exophoric

Consider now the following example:

17. Did **the** man come?

It is obvious that some parameter of identification renders **the man** definite. However, unlike (15a–c), this definiteness cannot consist in the presence of **the man** in the material situational setting. The total semantic structure of this clause as that of (15d–e) prevents such an interpretation. (17) thus presents a complete contrast to the (14a–d) and a partial one to (15a–c). Access to the material situational setting would render the former totally transparent; such access would also provide some information regarding **books** and **stones** in (15a–c) to the extent that their physical presence on the interactive scene can be affirmed, although there may be some other parameter of definiteness which does not become accessible to the casual listener. In (17) the casual listener has no interpretation, as the meanings intended by **the** go completely beyond the here-and-now of the discourse. Whoever is able to supply the correct intended

meanings here must possess knowledge that goes beyond this interactive situation and this particular text——it is knowledge that is
mutually shared through common past experience. The nature of this
knowledge is such that it precludes casual listeners completely. Thus
the correct retrieval of the intended meanings of **the** in (17) argues
for the existence of interaction in the past, and for a consequent
rapport between the speaker and the addressee. This is not a public
form of discourse.

When the interpretation of the implicit device depends upon the
above type of shared knowledge, excluding 'outsiders' from the circle
of communication, it may be referred to as *restricted exophoric.*
Other examples of this type would be:

17a. Has she already left?
  b. Let's hope we have a better holiday.
  c. I can't find the book.

5.3.6 Formal exophoric

The three types of exophorics discussed so far all differ from that
exemplified below:

18a. What was John on about?
    Tell you later.

The second clause——functioning as response——contains the implicit device of ellipsis——more accurately that of Subject-ellipsis
(from now on S-ellipsis). The environments in which S-ellipsis
can occur in English are formally identifiable; further, the location of their interpretative source can also be specified by reference
to formal criteria. Here are a few examples of endophoric S-
ellipsis:

19a. John will put off the lights and **lock up the door.**
  b. Where's Agnes?
    Finishing her homework.
  c. My dad can't come today.
    Can't come! Whyever not?

The second clause of each example contains S-ellipsis. Endophoric S-
ellipsis occurs only in the second member of a pair of clauses, such
that the pair either constitutes a co-ordinate clause complex (Halliday 1982) or it acts as an adjacency pair. The S-segment for the
elliptical clause is always interpreted by reference to the S-segment
of the clause to which it is co-ordinated or which functions as its

initiating pair-part. An associated feature of S-ellipsis is that no other clause may intervene between it and the clause that contains its interpretative source unless the intervening clause can act as a mediate link (Halliday and Hasan 1976). Thus in (19c) the third clause **whyever not?** can be interpreted as **whyever can't your dad come?** through the mediation of **can't come** which is itself interpreted as **your dad can't come!** by reference to the initiating pair-part **my dad can't come today.**

When S-ellipsis is exophoric, as in (18a), the intended S-segment cannot be retrieved by reference to the first member of the adjacency pair, even when such a member is around. The non-elliptical version of (18a) is not **John will tell you later** but **I will tell you later.** How is such an interpretation arrived at?

It is not that **I** is the only item which could function as the intended S-segment, and is therefore supplied automatically by the listener. This is evident from:

18b. Like an apple?
     Yeah, thanks.

Here the non-elliptical version of the first member in the adjacency pair would be **would you like an apple?**

In English, the more precise meaning of the exophoric S-ellipsis is either the first or the second person pronoun—either **I** or **you.** There is a strong tendency to interpret such a clause as 'needing' a first person pronoun if the contextual function of the clause is some variety of statement. If, on the other hand, the elliptical clause has the contextual function of question, the tendency is to interpret the S-ellipsis as second person pronoun. (For further discussion and rationale see Halliday 1982). These tendencies for the interpretation of exophoric S-ellipsis are so strong, that even if a clause with such an ellipsis were encountered in an uncharacteristic environment— i.e. in isolation from its situational setting—the normal speaker would interpret the ellipsis in the manner indicated above—unless there is good reason for doing otherwise.

This qualification is required for two reasons. First, complications arise due to the peculiarities of monologue and such text forming strategies as rhetorical questions. Secondly, the possibility of a third person pronominal as the intended S-segment cannot be ruled out entirely.

The possibility of a third person pronoun functioning as the intended S-segment in exophoric ellipsis, I regard as a marked state of affairs. There are three reasons for holding this view. If the intended S-segment is indeed a third person pronoun, then:

(a) whatever this pronoun refers to situationally must be present on the interactive scene;
(b) the speaker must accompany the utterance with some body cue, e.g. eye-movement, to directly pin-point the situational referent;
(c) unless the semantic structure of the clause prohibits, in isolation from the material situational setting, the clause would be assigned I or you as the intended S-segment.

These points can be illustrated from a consideration of the following:

20a. Met Harry.
  b. Met Harry?
  c. Met Harry, I believe.

There is nothing in the lexicogrammatical form of (20a–b) which prevents it from being interpreted as she met Harry. However, the formal convention for the interpretation of the exophoric S-ellipsis is so strong, that in isolation (20a) would be interpreted as I met Harry and if question-ness can be indicated in some way for (20b) it would be interpreted as did you meet Harry? In (20c), however, the insertion of I believe renders improbable the interpretation of the S-ellipsis as either I or you. Thus it is almost by default that (20c) may be interpreted as some one other than the interactants met Harry as the speaker believes.

In discussing how our casual listener would arrive at the interpretation of exophoric S-ellipsis, we must make a distinction between the marked and the unmarked variety. When S-ellipsis is unmarked, the intended meaning of the implicit device is available to all normal speakers of English. To know English is to know how to 'fill out' the ellipsis in such clauses as tell you later and like an apple?. So, even without access to the material situational setting, the casual listener would know that the former clause means I will tell you later and the latter, would you like an apple?. True that in this case the casual listener would not know the identity of the interactants; even so the general meaning is clear enough—the pronouns concern the maker and the receiver of the text in question.

It is implied in the above account that unmarked S-ellipsis is largely a formal matter. In the first place the recognition of ellipsis itself is purely formal. In English there is a formal requirement that a major clause with the feature 'indicative' must have the function Subject. It is this requirement which forces us to consider like an apple? as elliptical; after all, we do not need to have you as the liker of apple any more than we need to have you as the minder of your own business for the clause mind your own business! The argument

that **you** in both may be said to be understood and therefore necessary to the interpretation of both appears an irrelevance. In the fairly
common utterance **someone's at the door**, the nominal group **the
door** is normally understood as **the front door**. However, this does
not permit us to treat **the door** as an elliptical nominal group. There
is no formal requirement in English that every nominal group must
have the element Classifier in it. The recognition of ellipsis is not
based on the perception of implied meanings for if this were the
case every linguistic string produced would be elliptical, since
implication is a constant condition of encoding. Metaphorically
speaking, implied meanings are like the proverbial coming events
whose shadow is cast before by the actually occurring linguistic
units. The reason for insisting upon an element Subject for (18a-b)
and (20a-b) is not that if there is any liking or minding to do then
there should be a mention of someone who does this liking and
minding; it is rather that all indicative clauses in English must have
the element Subject. The element itself is an output of the Mood
system (Berry 1975-7; Halliday 1970; Young 1980); and appropriately enough the clue to the interpretation of the ellipsis is provided by reference to the options in the same system. Both the
ellipsis and its interpretation are thus formulaic in nature, permitting
no really true variation; and both are controlled by the system of
English language almost right down to the last detail. For this reason
I shall refer to such ellipsis as *formal exophoric*. A formal exophoric
device is one whose interpretation is pre-determined by the language
system and permits no true variation in wording.

Marked S-ellipsis presents a contrast to the above situation,
although there are several points in common. For a casual listener
with access to the material situational setting, the interpretation of
this ellipsis is as easy as that of the unmarked one. But once visual
contact with the material situational setting is removed, the casual
listener is likely to fare worse in the case of marked S-ellipsis. In the
last resort, this happens because marked S-ellipsis is not a formulaic
thing; and moreover, the third person pronominals are very much
less determinate in meaning than the first and second person ones.
These points can be elaborated by using (20c) as the text in focus.

A casual listener, who simply overhears but cannot see the goings-
on, will deduce from the total semantic structure of (20c) **met Harry
I believe** that someone other than the speaker or listener met Harry.
Whereas being able to see would have rendered the ellipsis quite
transparent, the inability to see leaves the casual listener with a far
more diffuse interpretation of (20c) than that of (20a-b) under the
same circumstances. This is because marked S-ellipsis is not formulaic;

so there exists the possibility of true variation in its interpretation. When the intended S-segment is I or you, although one may not be certain of the identity of the situational beings to whom these pronouns refer, a generalized meaning *speaker of text* and *addressee of text* are readily available to the casual listener. When, however, the intended S-segment is neither of these, then in the first place selection must be made from the paradigm he, she, it, they. And once this selection is made, there still remains the fact that the semantics of the third person pronoun is expressible only negatively by reference to the speech roles; thus members of the paradigm refer to some entity which does not have a speech role in the text in focus. This leaves the field wide open, even when the semantic structure of the text might be such as to favour one single selection from the paradigm. For example, if we overhear:

20d. Doesn't look ripe.

we know that the only pronoun capable of functioning as S-segment here would be it. But unlike I and you, it can be given no definite general meaning. Marked S-ellipsis is then very much like those implicit devices exemplified by (14a–d). With full access to the material situational setting, the casual listener will find it totally transparent; when such access is withheld, it renders the implicit device opaque.

5.4 DEGREES OF IMPLICITNESS AND EXPLICITNESS

5.4.1 Encoding devices and degrees of implicitness

The discussion above (5.3.1–5.3.6) has demonstrated an important fact. When the question is asked: how easy is the access to the intended meanings of an implicit device?, the answer cannot be given simply in terms of formally defined categories to which the various implicit devices belong. Not all pronominals are equally easy to interpret, nor all S-ellipsis. The definite article the can function differently depending upon the environment in which it occurs. Thus the classification presented above cross-cuts the classification of implicit devices as belonging to the categories of reference, ellipsis, and substitution (Halliday and Hasan 1976). The total set of encoding devices so far discussed can be presented as a taxonomy, the various categories of which differ from each other in respect of what is needed for their precise interpretation (see Figure 5.1). Earlier I suggested (5.2.2 above) that the implicitness of strings is variable; in that context, I used a purely quantitative method for

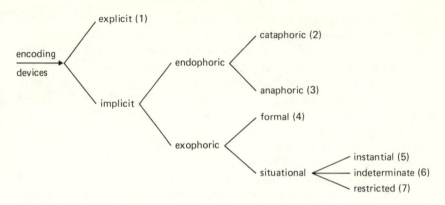

Fig. 5.1 Taxonomy of encoding devices

grading the degree of implicitness in a string: the larger the number of implicit devices in proportion to the explicit ones, the more implicit the string would be. In the light of the above remarks, it should be obvious that such quantitative grading is not the most reliable method. A more valid criterion for the grading of implicitness would be by reference to the requirements for interpretation. The greater the ease in interpreting the speaker's intended meanings, the less implicit the device. In using this criterion, the taxonomy in Figure 5.1 would be helpful.

The terminal nodes of this taxonomy yield a series (1–7). This series represents a cline of implicitness. On this continuum, the lowest number represents the least implicit device and the highest the most implicit ones, as shown in Figure 5.2.

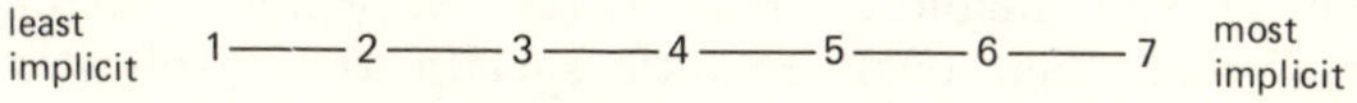

least
implicit   1 —— 2 —— 3 —— 4 —— 5 —— 6 —— 7   most
                                               implicit

Fig. 5.2 The cline of implicitness

Assuming normal speakers, the move from (1) to (7) is a move in the direction of an ever-narrowing circle of potentially successful interpreters; this is because the resources needed for such interpretation are increasingly more restrictive. Thus, the meanings of explicit devices (1) are available to every normal, mature speaker of English: the circle is the widest. With endophoric devices (2,3), this circle is reduced; it now covers only those who have access to the relevant part of the discourse. For (2), the relevant part of the discourse is expected to be more contiguous with the device than it would be with (3). With formal exophoric (4), this circle is further reduced; although the knowledge of language itself allows a partial interpretation, its precise intended meanings become fully available only when the listener has access to the material situational setting. This circle is likely to be much narrower than that for (2) and (3). Where instantial exophorics (5) are concerned, unless the listener has access to the material stituational setting, the devices would remain opaque; the interpretation that the casual listener might provide under such a situation would be far more diffuse than that for (4). So the circle of successful interpreters is rendered narrower still. In the case of indeterminate exophorics (6), access to material situational setting will permit some interpretation, but it is not necessary that even with such access the casual listener has understood all that there was to understand. Restricted exophoric (7) logically implies the narrowest circle; neither the knowledge of language nor the knowledge of the material situational setting is sufficient for a correct interpretation. As Bernstein puts it, one must be keyed into the relevant context; and this can happen through shared experience such that it generates a considerable amount of empathy.

5.4.2 Inherent grading of implicit devices

A new dimension can be added to the above grading of implicitness, by enquiring how far an implicit device provides clues about the area in which its more precise intended meaning may be located. The greater the detail with which this area can be stated, the narrower and better defined it is, the less implicit the device would be.

As a starting point we may consider the first and second person pronouns. It is justifiable to claim the lowest degree of implicitness for these since their own semantic specification explicates them fully; the only element of uncertainty is the particularity of the situational referent. In fact, the same claim can be made for all those implicit devices which involve 'textual deixis' by taking the text and its setting as their point of departure. Thus here, there, this, that, now have the lowest degree of implicitness.

The above situation contrasts with that of the third person pronouns (see also 5.3.6 above). The area from which the meaning of the third person pronoun may be retrieved is not as narrow as that for the above. Yet the semantic specification of he, she, it provides clues about the possible referents for these devices; under normal conditions he can only be co-referential with some item whose underlying semantic configuration includes [HUMAN; MALE; ONE;

NON-INTERACTANT]. Thus, inherently, the three singular third person pronouns are more transparent in their meaning than **they**, whose own semantic specification is much reduced as it contains [ONE+; NON-INTERACTANT].

In fact the inherent implicitness of **they** is greater than that of the nominal substitute **one/ones**. Any substitutable noun must have the underlying options [COUNTABLE; NON-UNIQUE] in addition to the two mentioned for **they**. Thus **I'll take these ones** cannot be said of **milk**, **tea**, and **sugar** though it may be said of cartons of milk, packets of tea, and bags of sugar. Similarly we can't say **here are John, Jim and Stanley. I'll take these ones with me** with **these ones** referring to **John, Jim, and Stanley**, though it is fine to say **I'm not worried about these three boys; I can take these ones with me—it's the others I can't find room for.** The inherent implicitness of the verbal substitute **do** is much greater by comparison, as there are only a few verbs that it cannot substitute (see Halliday and Hasan 1976).

The definite article **the** surpasses all the above-mentioned devices as in its inherent implicitness (see 5.3.1, 5.3.4 and 5.3.5). However because it cannot occur by itself, the modified noun itself can function as a clue-provider (see example 16a–d).

Perhaps the inherent implicitness is the greatest in the case of non-formulaic ellipsis. This claim is based on two observations. First, there can be instances, especially at the rank of clause, where simply by looking at the syntagm one cannot decide whether or not it is elliptical. I am not suggesting that in normal language use this creates any problem, since obviously here there is the entire dynamics of discourse to assist the listener. But this is not less true of **she, he, they**, etc. as implicit devices in normal language use. In talking about the inherent implicitness of the device, I am examining each as an isolate. And from this point of view there can be little doubt that by itself a clause such as **turn off the lights** does not appear elliptical. It would however be elliptical if we perceive it in relation to **John can tidy up, turn off the lights, and lock the doors.** Secondly, the general area from which the intended meanings might be retrieved is indicated by the internal properties of the elliptical string itself. Just as in the case of **the**, the modified noun is potentially a provider of clues to interpretation, so also in ellipsis, the rest of the syntagm assists in locating the intended meaning. This can be seen clearly from the following example:

21. If it had pleased them they would have told you. It didn't—so, naturally, they didn't—

Keeping the above discussion in mind, we can construct a cline of inherent implicitness. On this cline, the lowest degree of implicitness would be represented by the first/second person pronoun, and the highest by non-formulaic ellipsis. Using one item as representative of each category in question, the cline of inherent implicitness may be presented as in Figure 5.3.

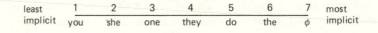

Fig. 5.3 The cline of inherent implicitness

5.4.3 Inherent grading of explicit devices

It seems necessary to draw attention to an aspect of explicit devices if only to provide a reason for not discussing them any further. These devices can be ranged on a continuum from general to specific; that is to say, explicit devices vary in the degree of specificity of meaning. This attribute is the recognized basis for the construction of lexical taxonomy. The terms 'implicit' and 'explicit' run parallel to 'general' and 'specific' in one important respect: the more implicit a device, the less precise the meaning it conveys; equally, the more general a device, the less precise the meaning it conveys. The line between the lowest degree of implicitness and the highest degree of generality is blurred; none the less, there is a qualitative difference between the two.

There can be no doubt that as we move along the series **thing, creature, animal, horse, foal, colt, yearling,** there is a reduction in generality and a proportionate increase in the specificity of meaning. **Thing** being the most general item in English even forms part of a composite implicit expression e.g. in **the silly thing;** here I am concerned with its other uses. The basic difference between **thing** and an implicit device e.g. **it** is that when the speaker uses an implicit device, at least he himself is quite clear about the more precise intended meaning; also, he expects his addressee too to perceive this meaning. The same claim cannot be made about the use of **thing.** Compare:

22a. Do you see that thing over there? What is it?
   b. Do you see it? What's that thing over there?

In (22a) the nature of whatever is being pointed out is not clear to the speaker; this is shown by the generality of **thing,** which commits the speaker to no more than the pointed-out being an object. Thereafter it can be used with the meaning: the afore-mentioned object. (22b) is odd because the use of it creates an effect of the speaker knowing more than the following clause gives him credit for; as the text stands it and **that thing over there** are co-referential. If the same two clauses are read with an **and** between them, which negates the co-referentiality, the text would be quite normal.

The cline presented by **thing, creature . . . . . yearling** can be related to the cline as shown in Figure 5.4. The continuum between

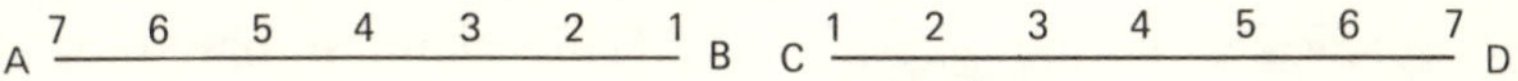

```
  7   6   5   4   3   2   1       1   2   3   4   5   6   7
A ─────────────────────────── B  C ─────────────────────────── D
```

Fig. 5.4 The relation between least specific and least implicit

(A-D) represents all the encoding devices, (A) being the implicit end, and (D) the explicit one. (A-B) represent only the implicit devices ranging from (A): most implicit to (B): least implicit; (C-D) repre-sent only the explicit devices, ranging from (C): the least specific— i.e. general—to (D) the most specific. The gap between (B) and (C) indicates the qualitative difference between the two categories of encoding devices. Hopefully Figure 5.4 shows clearly that despite the nearness between the notions of implicitness and non-specificity, the two are not identical. However, as example (16a-d) showed, the occurrence of general devices can affect access to meaning.

5.4.4 On establishing degrees of implicitness

It may be concluded from the discussion in this section that to talk of implicit and explicit ways of saying as if it were a simple binary distinction would be to create yet another non-existent dichotomy. The three variables—quantitative, based on the proportion of implicit to explicit devices; qualitative, based on resources for access to the intended meanings; and the inherent implicitness and generality of the devices—operate together to produce what we impres-sionistically describe as highly implicit, somewhat implicit, or entirely explicit. In the comparison of ways of speaking between middle-class English and Urdu speakers, only the latter two qualita-tive variables will be considered in determining the degree of implicit-ness. The quantitative criterion will be ignored since it can only be employed on the basis of a systematic analysis of a large amount of corpus.

5.5 ENGLISH SEMANTIC STYLE

5.5.1 The semantic style of English

If semantic style is a characteristic way of saying and meaning, then the defining attributes of this style should be present in most natural verbal interaction. Exceptions, where the characteristic semantic style is not used, will be significantly fewer; moreover it should be possible to state clearly how these exceptions can be defined.

On this definition of characteristic semantic style, I would suggest that the predominant semantic style for the educated middle-class English speaker is the explicit one. This claim is based on two observations: first, the system of English itself does not permit the possibility of using the logically most implicit means of encoding; secondly, such implicitness as is permitted by the system can be used only in few and well-defined environments, thus indicating that it is a departure from the norm. These points are developed below.

5.5.2 Degrees of permissible implicitness in English

In the discussion of the significant degrees of implicitness, we need not concern ourselves with devices other than those functioning exophorically. The endophoric devices are only temporarily implicit, so much so that the listener is typically unaware of their occurrence so long as the relevant co-text is available. And even among the exophorics, the formal exophoric is a border-line case (see 5.3.6). The logically highest degree of implicitness would be reached if ellipsis could function as a restricted exophoric. (See Figures 5.2 and 5.3.) If my analysis is correct, English does not permit such ellipsis —when ellipsis is not endophoric, it is typically instantial exophoric. Thus the logically highest possible degree of implicitness is not permitted to occur in English.

The next degree would be represented by the functioning as a restricted exophoric. The occurrence of such the is permitted. Thus this could be regarded as the highest permissible degree of implicitness in English. Since the substitutes do not function as restricted exophoric, we are left with the and the third person pronominals that can function in this way. These same devices can also function as instantial exophoric.

I have argued that the instantial exophoric is rendered quite transparent to anyone who happens to have full access to the material situational setting. We can claim then that in English there are only two significant degrees of implicitness: the optimal and the non-optimal. The optimal is achieved with the functioning of the device as a restricted exophoric. However, a large proportion of the implicit devices are prevented from functioning in this manner. The system of English language does not favour the optimal degree of implicitness. The non-optimal degree of implicitness is fairly low, and it is open to all implicit devices. Thus the system of English language may be said to favour this kind of implicitness.

These generalizations hold for all varieties of English. The degree of implicitness that can be achieved in English is much lower for all varieties, not just middle-class English, than that which could logically have been possible. This is partly what would be meant by the claim that the predominant semantic style of English is explicit. It isn't simply that the English speaker *would* not, but rather that he *could not*, speak as implicitly as the Urdu speaker, even if he tried—the system of his language will not permit him to do so.

5.5.3 Environments for the operation of implicit styles

That the implicit style is the marked style for most speakers of English and particularly for the middle-class members is also borne out by the fact that the environments in which implicit style may be employed appropriately are few and very clearly specifiable.

Let us take the non-optimal degree—that where the devices are used as instantial exophorics. This kind of implicitness occurs characteristically in face-to-face encounters. This, it might be argued, is quite logical: the instantial exophoric is rendered transparent if one has access to the situational setting. In their setting the meanings of **don't** and **have some more** are quite obvious; divorced from this setting, their meaning is opaque. It is, therefore, quite appropriate that their higher occurrence should be associated with an environment which gives total access to the material situational setting.

The frequency of the instantial exophorics is higher still in a face-to-face encounter where the relationship between the interactants is intimate. Thus we can say that the more informal the tenor, the more likely the middle-class English speaker would be to use this kind of implicitness. However, this aspect of the correlation cannot be said to be logical in nature. If it is true that the casual listener with full access to the material situational setting would be able to interpret the instantial exophorics almost as successfully as the intended addressee, then it cannot be maintained that intimacy between the interactants is a logical requirement for its more

frequent occurrence. It seems to me that an understanding of the
semiotic control on the optimally implicit style might provide
a rationale for the correlation between informal tenor and higher
frequency of instantial exophorics.

The optimal degree of implicitness, where the devices are used as
restricted exophorics, can be employed only in those environments
where the social distance between the interactants is minimal (Hasan
1973, 1978, 1980). A relationship of intimacy, if not necessarily
that of informality, is logically required, since the interpretation of
meanings rests on shared knowledge which is a product of consistent
past interaction. It is this aspect of the restricted exophorics which
excludes strangers and casual listeners.

It is probably useful to separate the assumptions that accompany
the use of restricted exophorics from the conditions favourable to
its successful interpretation. A speaker employing such a style of
speaking assumes that his addressee is 'keyed into' the discourse, that
their mental set is the same and that there is no danger of ambiguity
or misunderstanding—in short, the speaker assumes that the addressee knows what he is talking about. Such expectations cannot be
entertained regarding every member of one's speech community over
a wide range of contexts. Obviously, then, the circle of potential
addressees is likely to be limited to those in-group members with
whom a certain degree of empathy is experienced. This assumption
of the close mental set, of empathy, is a logical necessity to the
sensical use of restricted exophorics. Their successful interpretation
depends upon the correctness of these assumptions; if the assumptions were not well founded, the implicit style would be a constant
source of frustration to both parties. There can of course be occasions when although the assumption of empathy is correct in principle, the interpretation is not successful because the addressee's
attention is being claimed by some other matter. I do not think that
this affects the points being made here; such sporadic failures of
communication are likely to occur in any style of communication,
not just the implicit one.

Social distance itself is variable in degree (Hasan 1973, 1978,
1980); there are intermediate degrees of intimacy felt for an utter
stranger or for one's own mother, wife, or close friend. It is, however, best to talk of social distance in comparative terms without
referring to a relationship as the measure for the degree; this is
because across the cultures the kind of intimacy that may exist
between spouses, parents and children, or friends can be qualitatively different (Hsu 1971). It can be claimed that the more minimal
the social distance between the interactants, the more likely the

occurrence of restricted exophorics. Thus a frequent use of such exophorics is indicative of the fact that the interactants habitually interact in wider areas of the living of life. This style of speaking is, then, indexical of a qualitatively different social relation (Bernstein 1971).

It is my tentative suggestion that the correlation between the higher frequency of instantial exophorics and informal tenor is a symbolic means of construing closeness of relationship. The efficacy of this symbolism depends upon the semiotics of the optimally implicit style. Because of the logical relationship between the restricted exophoric and the closeness of social ties, the former tends to be seen as the outward manifestation of the latter. Instantial exophorics are an attempt to create the semblance of this reality. There are many ways in which language makes up our world for us —not simply naming existing objects, processes, and states, but actually creating them. Despite the long philosophical tradition, the primacy of the onomastic function of language is highly suspect. Language is useful to social man not because it names all the pre-existing phenomena in the world, but because it actually creates the most significant ones. 'The limits of my language mean the limits of my world' (Wittgenstein 1921).

5.5.4 Concluding remarks on English semantic styles

I conclude from the above discussion that the characteristic semantic style in English is the explicit one. The very fact of speaking English forces one toward explicitness rather than implicitness. Further, this is even more so with regard to the educated middle-class English speakers. To say that one is a middle-class English speaker is to say that for the most part one talks so that one's meanings are easily available to anyone present at the interactive scene. The assumption of shared knowledge and reliance upon it, which is a logical necessity for the successful operation of implicit style, is not encouraged in the majority of interactive environments. Ambiguity is an ever-present threat, therefore; explicitization is an imperative. There are very few contexts in which the middle-class English speaker is free to assume complete rapport with others of his kind. The similitude of beliefs, attitudes, and values (Durkheim 1947) which would make each one of us as like the other as possible, despite our physical discreteness, is not to be taken for granted. So, to put it sentimentally, the universe is a lonely place, where each one of us is an island unto himself.

If in a background such as I have described above—especially

with reference to the total language system—we find a section of
the speech community whose predominant orientation is to the
implicit style of speaking, we must ask *why*. What conditions obtain
for this section of the community which guide the speakers' options
to paths in the language system, which are not favoured by the
members of other sections of this same speech community. The
variation is not a matter of shame; nor does it call for an indignant
championship of the variant section (Labov 1970). To me it seems
that there is just as much condescension in saying that 'they' are
like 'us', as there is in maintaining that 'we' are better than 'them'.
'Us' and 'them' are culturally created realities, as are also the standards of good, bad, and better. They cannot be altered by a simple
denial of their existence; they must be analysed and understood,
if we are to redress the balance in the monopoly of cultural values.
To recognize with Bernstein that the various styles of speaking
are socially created phenomena, which further the status quo of an
established power structure, is to be pointed in the direction of
exposing the sources of cultural monopoly. Thus it is meaningful
to ask: what creates this assumption of rapport in 'them' which is
so conspicuously missing from 'our' own social universe? I propose
to throw some light on this problem by comparing the dominant
middle-class English semantic style with the Urdu one.

5.6 URDU SEMANTIC STYLE

5.6.1 Implicitness in Urdu

I have developed the categories of implicitness and my main argu-
ments by reference to English, in the hope that it may lead to an
easier understanding of facts relating to Urdu. In talking about the
patterns of implicitness in Urdu, I shall have to make statements
regarding its lexicogrammatical structure. Such statements are inci-
dental to the main purpose of this chapter and it will not be possible
to include justification for my claims at each point.

My strategy will be to start with an examination of the logically
highest degree of implicitness—that which would arise from a substantial use of restricted exophoric ellipsis. If I can show that this
type of implicitness is permitted in Urdu, and that it is not counter-
balanced by turning ellipsis to either formal or instantial exophoric,
then I shall have shown that the potential for implicitness is higher
in Urdu than it is in English. The system of Urdu language itself could
then be said to allow a higher degree of implicitness to its speakers
than that which is permitted by the system of English language.

My second step would be to enquire into the range of environments where this higher degree of implicitness might be employed by Urdu speakers. If I can show that such a style of speaking is characteristically employed by Urdu speakers over a wide range of contexts, I shall have proved that not only does the system permit a higher degree of implicitness, but also the speakers make wide use of it; and therefore the dominant Urdu style is the implicit one.

Finally I shall raise two questions: first, how does this style relate to the prevalent semiotic style and what organizing concepts may be at work in maintaining this parallelism; secondly, what do these findings say about that sub-section of English speakers who are orientated to the implicit style of speaking?

5.6.2 S-ellipsis in Urdu

It would be useful to compare the patterns of S-ellipsis across the two languages, but there is the initial problem of determining what, if anything, the element S of English corresponds to in Urdu. The traditional accounts of Urdu grammar are not very clear on this issue; thus in the traditional description of the grammar of the language there appears to exist no category with the exact value of the English Subject. The term closest to Subject appears to be '*məsnəd yləh*' (Fateh Mohammad Khan 1945: 195 f.) which together with '*məsnəd*' renders a clause potentially a 'complete unit of discourse'. 'Məsnəd' is defined as that which is related to—or pertains to— something; the thing to which it pertains is defined as 'm ə sn ə d yl ə h'. We are further told that while the latter is always realized by a nominal unit, the former can be realized by a nominal and/or verbal unit. This makes it sound as if 'məsnəd yləh' and 'məsnəd' correspond exactly to the distinction made by Subject and Predicate, respectively. However, such an interpretation would not be quite accurate. The two categories recognized in the traditional Urdu grammars are said to apply only to that class of clauses, regarding which the question of truth or falsehood could be sensibly raised. So, reasonably enough, not only the imperative but also the interrogative —among many other clause classes—are specifically excluded from this category.[2] In

23. **twm** kəb ləndən gəĩ?
    you when London went?
    when did **you** go to London?

twm (you) is not a 'm ə sn ə d yl ə h'; nor is there a 'm ə sn ə d' in this clause. Rather than being diverted into a lengthy discussion of this issue, I shall follow modern grammatical descriptions in affirming that a category comparable to the English Subject can be recognized usefully for Urdu as well (Kachru 1966; Verma 1961; Hasan 1972). First, I shall stipulate which segment of the clause is in question when we use the term Subject to refer to it. The statement would read as follows:

That segment of the Urdu clause is comparable to the S-segment of the English one, which has the privilege of number–gender–person concord with the verbal group realizing the element Process in the clause. The sole exception to this, are clauses where a nominal group with post-position 'ne' is either actually present or is potentially insertable. In this latter class of clauses the nominal group with the post-position 'ne' is comparable to the S-segment.

Here are a few examples; the S-segment in each case is underlined both in Urdu and the English clause-rank translations:

24a. ləRki   dal   pəka rəhi həy
     girl   lentils cook   ing   is
     (the) girl is cooking (some) lentils
   b. ləRki cavəl pəka rəhi həy
      girl   rice   cook ing   is
      (the) girl is cooking (some) rice
   c. dal   pəkai   ja rəhi həy
      lentils cooked go ing   is
      lentils are being cooked
   d. cavəl pəkaya ja rəha həy
      rice   cooked go ing is
      rice is being cooked
   e. ləRki ne   dal   pəkai
      girl   lentils cooked
      (the) girl cooked (some) lentils
   f. ləRki   ne cavəl pəkaya
      girl   rice   cooked
      (the) girl cooked (some) rice
   g. admi   dal   pəka rəha həy
      man   lentils cook ing   is
      (the) man is cooking (some) lentils
   h. admi cavəl pəka rəha həy
      man   rice cook ing   is
      (the) man is cooking (some) rice

Although the above examples represent only a very small sub-set of the total paradigm, they substantiate the points made above, especially if the information is added that in (24 e–f), ləRki could

be replaced by **admi**, without causing any change in the meaning
except that resulting from the lexical difference between the two
items.

It is, of course, comparatively easy to establish which segment of
the Urdu clause is most like the S-segment of the English one; it is
quite a different matter to validate the recognition of Subject as
a descriptive category in Urdu grammar. Yet such motivation must
be present if we claim S-ellipsis as a significant fact in Urdu. If there
is such an element of structure in the Urdu clause, what is its
function? What systemic options is it related to? And how may
its semantic value be determined? To begin with we may state
clearly that neither in English nor in Urdu is the element S an output
of the Transitivity system; for Urdu this should be obvious from
a comparison of (24a) and (c). In agreement with Halliday, I have
argued that S in English is the output of the Mood system; and
although there are crucial differences, I would propose that the same
is true of Urdu. Before stating the evidence for this conclusion, it is
important to add that there are two separate aspects to be examined:
first, the justification for the recognition of the element S; and
secondly, the actual presence, absence, and position of the S-segment
in the syntagm.

Essentially the function of S in Urdu is the same as that in
English; it acts as 'something by reference to which the proposi-
tion can be affirmed or denied' (Halliday 1982). In English, this
is what underlies the systematic behaviour of tag questions. In
Urdu, there is only one invariable tag **hɔy na** (is not: isn't it), however the principle that 'the subject is responsible for the success
of the proposal' (Halliday, ibid.) holds good. It is certainly the
'resting point of the argument', so that it always functions as
the point of reference for raising any queries about the message.
A consideration of the following examples will illustrate the above
points:

25a. <u>hamyd</u>   nɔwkrani   nɔhī laya
    <u>Hamid</u> maid-servant   not   brought
    <u>Hamid</u> didn't bring the maidservant

  b. nɔwkrani   <u>hamyd</u> nɔhi̇   laya
    maid-servant <u>Hamid</u>   not   brought
    the maid-servant <u>Hamid</u> didn't bring (i.e. it was not Hamid
    who brought her)

  c. hamyd se   <u>nɔwkrani</u> nɔhī lai   gɔi
    Hamid by maid-servant not brought went
    <u>the maid-servant</u> was not brought by Hamid

d. nəwkrani   hamyd se nəhĩ lai   gəi
   maid-servant Hamid by not brought went
   the maid-servant was not brought by Hamid

The segment in each clause is underlined; that neither order nor
participant status affects Subject-ness is also obvious. However, since
S is the resting point of the argument, if the propositions are to be
debated then S must serve as the point of reference. Suppose one
wishes to contradict the statements (25a-d), then the contradiction
for (25a-b) will be as follows:

26 i. laya to
       brought emphatic particle
       did bring (i.e. he did)
   ii. kəhã nəhi laya
       where not brought
       where didn't bring (i.e. of course he did)
   iii. kəyse nəhi laya
        how   not brought
        how didn't bring (i.e. of course he did)
   iv. laya   kyõ nəhi
       brought why not
       why didn't bring (i.e. of course he did)

(26i-iv) can all function as contradictions of (25a-b), although
with some differences in emphasis. This latter point need not concern us here; but it should be noted that in each case, the concord
pattern of the contradiction quite clearly shows **Hamid** to be the
central reference point. If this is compared with the contradictions for (25c-d), we find that the pattern of concord 'picks
up' **nawkrani** as the resting point of the argument. Compare (26i-iv)
with (27i-iv):

27 i. lai   to   gəi
       brought emphatic particle went
       did get brought (i.e. she did (get brought))
   ii. kəhâ nəhî   lai   gəi
       where not brought went
       where didn't get brought (i.e. of course she did (get brought))
   iii. kəyse nəhi lai   gəi
        how   not brought went
        how didn't get brought (i.e. of course she did (get brought))
   iv. lai   kyõ nəhi gəi
       brought why not went
       why didn't get brought (i.e. of course she did get brought))

Although the experiential meanings of (25a–d) are the same, there-fore contradicting one of these is experientially tantamount to contradicting the others, these patterns of contradiction are not exchangeable. Thus while (25e–f) make a good exchange, (25 g–h) are definitely odd:

25e. -hamyd nɔwkrani nɔhĩ laya (see (25a) for translation)
    -laya to   (see (26i) for translation)
  f. -hamyd se nɔwkrani nɔhĩ lai gɔi (see (25c) for translation)
    -lai to gɔi   (see (27i) for translation)
  g. -hamyd nɔwkrani nɔhĩ laya
    -lai to gɔi
  h. -hamyd se nɔwkrani nɔhĩ lai gɔi
    -laya to

Clearly this pattern obtains because S is the point of reference. When the contradictions are switched around, the alteration in the concord pattern indicates a segment as S which cannot so function for g and h; hence the oddity of the latter two exchanges. The point is brought out even more dramatically if we consider a clause where the S-segment is a pronoun referring to one of the interactants, as in:

28. hɔm ytna   kam nɔhĩ kɔrte
   I   so much work not do
   I don't do so much work (i.e. I don't work so hard)

Imagine that the I here refers to the author. The relevant properties of the S-segment then would be: first person, singular, feminine. Its ordinary contradiction would be:

28i. kɔrti   to   ho
   do   emph. part. are
   do do (i.e. (you) do)

Here the verbal group through its concord points to a S-segment whose properties are: second person, singular, feminine. Given the nature of the exchange, this is exactly how it should work.

It is significant that even in clauses where the S-segment is a nominal group with post-position ne, if the natural context permits, the pattern of concord will change to point to the S. Consider the following:

29. -ap   ki lɔRik ne ye drama nɔhĩ dekha nɔ?
    you of girl   this play not saw no
    your daughter didn't see this play, did she?
    -nɔhĩ kɔl   dekhe gi
    not tomorrow see will
    no, tomorrow will see (i.e. no, (she) will see it tomorrow)

In the initiating turn the concord is not with the ne-group—as it never is—but in the second turn, where the tense of the verbal group permits this, the person, number and gender concord is with ləRki. We also find such 'switching' of concord in co-ordinated pair with ellipsis:

30. <u>kwlsum</u> ne bəRi mətanət se mwjhe <u>dekha</u> əwr phyr
     Kulsoom   very seriousness with me looked-at and then
     Kulsoom looked at me very seriously and then

     əpni kapi pər <u>jhwk gəi</u>
     her note-book at bent went
     bent (her head) over her notebook

                                                  (Ishfaq Ahmed: 181)

It appears then that the concord which ties the elements S and Predicator in Urdu is not simply an empty formalism, but is semantically motivated. In English the centrality of the element S to the clause is reflected in the significance that must be attached to its actual presence and its position in the syntagm; in Urdu, the reflection of this centrality is the pattern of concord, which points to the identity of the S (see below, for further remarks). Hopefully, this discussion shows that despite differences between the English and Urdu Subject, there exists sufficient similarity between the two to permit valid comparison.

Although the element S is the output of the Mood system in Urdu, the actual presence, absence and position of the S-segment in the clause is not determined by the Mood system. The presence or absence of the S-segment is largely a realization of the options in the Information system, while its position in the syntagm is related to the Key system and to the Theme system. I shall not concern myself with problems relating to the position of the S-segment, but I do need to say something about the conditions which control its appearance or absence from the clause. The discussion will be largely in terms of the Information system, though the system of Theme too affects aspects of this.

Two elements which are the output of the Information system are Given and New; together they make up a structure called 'information unit'. Under normal conditions, the information unit is coextensive with one clause. As elaboration on these statements it is best to quote from Halliday 1982):

The information unit is what its name implies: a unit of information. Information, as . . . used here, is a process of interaction between what is already known and what is new or unpredictable . . . . It is the interplay of new and not new that generates information in the linguistic sense. Hence the information unit is a structure made up of two functions, the New and Given.

In the idealized form each information unit consists of a Given element accompanied by a New element. But there are two conditions of departure from this principle. One is that discourse has to start somewhere, so there can be discourse initiating units consisting of a New element only. The other is that by its nature the Given is likely to be 'phoric'—referring to something already present in the verbal or non-verbal context; and one way of achieving phoricity is through ellipsis, a grammatical form in which certain features are not realized in the structure.

One of the conditions of departure from the ordinary structure of the information unit is met with quite frequently in Urdu: it is the achievement of phoricity through S-ellipsis as a (partial) manifestation of the element Given. S-ellipsis in Urdu is the output of this systemic option, though it should be noted that the S-segment of a clause is not always realizationally associated with the element New, since it could be the (partial) realization of unmarked Theme, especially when it precedes both Complement and Predicate. The fact that S-ellipsis in Urdu is controlled by a systemic option does not weaken the ground for its comparison with S-ellipsis in English. This is obvious from the true meaning of the elements Given and New. To quote Halliday again (1982):

The significant variable is: information that is presented by the speaker as recoverable (Given) or not recoverable (New) to the listener. What is treated as recoverable may be so because it has been mentioned before; but that is not the only possibility. It may be something that is in the situation, like I and you; or in the air, so to speak; or something that is not around at all but that the speaker wants to present as Given for rhetorical purposes. The meaning is: this is not news. Likewise, what is treated as non-recoverable may be something that has not been mentioned; but it may be something unexpected, whether previously mentioned or not. The meaning is: attend to this; this is news . . . .

These are precisely the possibilities of interpretation we have been considering for the implicit devices: either they are interpreted endophorically or exophorically; if exophorically, either through some bit of the situational setting or through shared knowledge. Urdu S-ellipsis does not present any contrast in these respects. It acts like an implicit device; it is quite beside the point that it is itself (partially) motivated by the options in the system of Information.

Endophoric S-ellipsis is far more frequent in Urdu than it is in English. In the latter case, the environment can be enumerated very simply (see 5.3.6 above); for Urdu, it is easier to formulate the principle negatively: S-ellipsis cannot occur wherever the S-segment would form part of New or contrastive information. Although endophoric S-ellipsis is not my primary concern here, an extract

from a short story is presented below just to give an idea of how
frequent this pattern is in Urdu:

31. təbyət   ke badshah the thwmhare nana; dyl mẽ
    temperament of king was your grand-dad; heart in
    by temperament he was a king, your grand-dad; if (he)

    kysi ciz ki Than   li to phyr wse pura kər
    any thing of determine take then it finish do
    made up his mind to do something then (he) would draw breath

    ke hi dəm lia. həm   lakh   sər marẽ,
    after breath took I thousand head beat,
    only after finishing it. I might try my utmost,

    mənnətẽ xwshamdẽ kərẽ, tane uləhne   dẽ, məgər
    prayers flatteries do taunts   give but
    (I) might cajole or pray, (I) might even taunt, but

    vo vəhi kwch kərte jo wnhe pəsənd hota.
    he that some do which him liked was
    he only did whatever pleased him.

    gəRh shənkər mẽ nayb təhsildar the; ytni bəRi
    Garh Shanker in deputy collector was; such big
    (He) was deputy revenue collector in Garh Shanker; such a big

    həveli   do bhõyse ek ghoRi car kwtte
    residence two buffaloes one mare four dogs
    residence, two buffaloes, one mare and four dogs [it carried].

    kysi ne   a kər shəgufa choR dia kə KəŋgaRe
    someone came did flower leave gave that Kangara
    someone just brought a tempting tale that a holy man has

    mẽ ek dərvesh ae hẽy.   jo   kəhte hẽy vəhi kər
    in a holy man come is. whatever say is that do
    come to Kangara. Whatever (he) says (he) actually

    dykhate hẽy; kysi se mylte nəhi; kysi ko mwrid
    show   is; anyone with meets not; someone disciple
    brings about; (he) doesn't meet anyone; (he) doesn't take

    nəhĩ bənate. vo to əysi batõ ke dyl se xwahã
    not makes. he such things of heart with desirous
    any disciples. he of course was very keen on such things

    the; jhəT ystifə lykh bheja . . .
    was; at once resignation wrote sent
    ; straight away (he) sent off his resignation . . .

                                        [Ishfaq Ahmed: p. 27]

The extract in (31) consists of 17 major clauses with 17 finite verbal groups. So, potentially, there could be 17 S-segments. However, only seven of these have an S-segment; the remaining 10 display S-ellipsis which is indicated by putting the intended S-segment in round brackets in the English translation.

5.6.3 Formal exophoric S-ellipsis in Urdu

The question may be raised whether S-ellipsis in Urdu does not simply function as formal exophoric, when it is not endophoric; after all, if there is concord between Subject and Predicator, then the latter must provide clues for the correct interpretation of the former. However, the situation is not as simple as this—and for several reasons.

First, there are clause types in which the concord obtains not between S and P but between P and Complement (as in 24 e–f above). Thus if we have an example, such as the second and the third clauses of the following:

32. mɔ̃y   ys   tɔrəh   ke   khane   se   bylkwl   ajyz   a   gəya;
    I   this kind   of   food   with   absolutely   sick   come   went;
    I am absolutely sick of this kind of food;

    dal   pəkai   to   cavəl   nəhĩ,   cavəl   pəkaya   to
    lentils   cooked   then   rice   not,   rice   cooked   then
    if (—) cook lentils then no rice, if (—) cook rice then

    dal   nəhĩ.
    lentils   not
    no lentils.

No clues are provided regarding the nature of the S-segment from the form of the P pəkai and pəkaya.

Even when concord obtains between S and P, as in the majority of cases, the form of the P-segment is not entirely unambiguous; thus it may permit not just one single invariant possibility but a range from which choice must be made. This is obvious from a comparison of the following two examples:

33. kəl   ja   rəhi   hũ   pətə   nəhĩ   kəb   vapəs   aũ   gi   əb
    tomorrow   go   ing   am   know   not   when   back   come   will   now
    (I) am going tomorrow, God knows when (I) will be back again now

34. kəl   ja   rəhe   hɔ̃y   pətə   nəhĩ   kəb   vapəs   aẽ   ge   əb
    tomorrow   go   ing   am   know   not   when   back   come   will   now

In (33), the P-segment is entirely unambiguous; it permits one single invariant interpretation, pointing to an S-segment which must have the following properties: first person, singular, feminine, formal. These requirements are met only by one item in the language—the pronoun mɔy. Thus the casual listener has no problem in understanding the speaker's meanings; further, note that the amount of information he would have on simply hearing (33) is more detailed than that he would have for (18a): **tell you later**. By contrast, it is not possible to provide one single translation for (34); the P-segment permits more than one option, and further complications arise from the nature of the Urdu pronominal system. Thus the following S-segments are permissible for (34):

34 i. ap kəl   ja rəhe hɔy . . . . . .
    <u>you</u> are going tomorrow
                         [ap = you: 2nd person, sing., masc., honorific]

    ii. həm kəl   ja rəhe hɔy . . . .
    <u>I/we</u> am/are going tomorrow . . . . .
                         [həm I: 1st person, sing., fem./masc., informal]
                         [həm we: 1st person, plural, fem./masc., informal]

    iii. <u>vo</u>   kəl   ja   rəhe   hɔy . . . . .
    <u>he/they</u> is/are going tomorrow . . . . .
                         [vo he: 3rd person, sing., masc., honorific]
                  [vo they: 3rd person, plural, masc., hono./non.hono.]

In (34), it is possible to insert any of the three pronouns **ap**, **həm** or **vo** as the S-segment. Urdu pronouns are unambiguous only with regard to the speech role (i.e. person) information; their number and gender is projected by the P-segment. Since in (34) this segment is not unambiguous, alternative possibilities of interpretation for **həm** and **vo** exist. A casual listener who simply overhears (34) is not likely to be able to interpret it without some additional clues.

Finally, unlike English it is not the case in Urdu that exophoric S-ellipsis must be interpreted as **I** if the clause has the function of statement and as **you** if the clause has the function of question. The discussion of (34) has hopefully demonstrated that clauses with the function of statement can be interpreted, at least in some environments, as having a first, second or third person as their intended S-segment. To consider clauses with the function of question, compare the following:

ii. zɔrə ydhər ao!
    little here come
    come here for a minute!

35 i. kəhã   cəli gəi?
    where walk went

iii. zɔrə ydhər bwlao!
    little here   call
    call (——) here for a minute!

(35i) may be interpreted as (a) **where have you got to?** in which case (iii) cannot follow it; the addressee of both (35i) and (ii) is the same person. It is also possible to interpret (35i) as (b) **where has/ have she/they got to?**; in this case (35iii) is not addressed to the same person, whose absence is the subject of comment in (35i). In other words, the clause with question function is not necessarily to be interpreted as if its intended S-segment is a second person pronoun.

For these reasons the stating of environments where exophoric S-ellipsis would simply belong to the category 'formal' is not as simple for Urdu as it is for English. Space does not permit a detailed discussion, but some general tendencies may be noted about the kind of indications provided by the P-segment for the interpretation of S-ellipsis:

(i) The P-segment provides a clearer indication to the nature of the intended S-segment, if the number selection is singular; greater neutralization of person and gender occurs when the number is plural.

(ii) Even with a singular selection, the gender of the S-segment is indicated unambiguously more frequently than its person status; second person status is indicated invariantly with greater frequency than the first or third person status.

(iii) An invariant S-segment is indicated more frequently if the primary tense selection is present, rather than future, rather than past.

By implication, then, the optimal environment for the functioning of S-ellipsis as formal exophoric is where the P-segment of the clause unmistakably displays a singular number and a primary present tense. This possibility will be considerably reduced if the tense selection is future, and even more reduced where the tense is past. Irrespective of tense, S-ellipsis is less likely to be formal exophoric if the number selection is even potentially plural. These predictions can be checked from Table 5.1, where the lexical verb is **become** (hona) and **walk**

Table 5.1 Partial paradigm of verbal groups

		singular (I: mɛ̃y; you: twm; he/she/it: vo)		plural (we: həm; you: twmlog; they: vo)		
		(i) M	(ii) F	(iii) M	(iv) F	
First person (I)	present	hota, cəlta / hũ, hũ	hoti, cəlti / hũ, hũ	hote, cəlte / hãy, hãy	hote, cəlte / hãy, hãy	(a) (b)
	future	hũ, cəlũ / ga, ga	hũ, cəlũ / gi, gi	hõ, cəlẽ / ge, ge	hõ, cəlẽ / ge, ge	(c) (d)
	past	hua, cəla / (tha)	huĩ, cəli / (thi)	hue, cəle / (the)	hue, cəle / (the)	(e) (f)
Second person (II)	present	hote, cəlte / ho, ho	hoti, cəlti / ho, ho	hote, cəlte / ho, ho	hoti, cəlti / ho, ho	(a) (b)
	future	ho, cəlo / ge, ge	ho, cəlo / gi, gi	ho, cəlo / ge, ge	ho, cəlo / gi, gi	(c) (d)
	past	hue, cəle / (the)	huĩ, cəli / (thĩ)	hue, cəle / (the)	huĩ, cəli / (thĩ)	(e) (f)
Third person (III)	present	hota, cəlta / hɛy, hɛy	hoti, cəlti / hɛy, hɛy	hote, cəlte / hãy, hãy	hoti, cəlti / hãy, hãy	(a) (b)
	future	ho, cəle / ga, ga	ho, cəle / gi, gi	hõ, cəlẽ / ge, ge	hõ, cəlẽ / gi, gi	(c) (d)
	past	hua, cəla / (tha)	huĩ, cəli / (thi)	hue, cəle / (the)	huĩ, cəli / (thĩ)	(e) (f)

(cɔlna). This table relates only to the P-segments in indicative clauses where the verbal group is positive. A great deal of neutralization results when the verbal group is negative and/or the tense system applicable is a non-indicative one. A further source of neutralization is to be found in the distinctions made by reference to the systems of 'formality' and 'honorifics' which are applicable to the Urdu pronouns. This invariably has the effect of rendering the P-segment with a potentially plural selection more ambivalent with regard to person, gender and number (see the discussion of example (34) above).

It was important to go into this degree of detail in order to bring home the realization that in Urdu, exophoric S-ellipsis *cannot* function as formal exophoric in a wide variety of environments. If then, S-ellipsis *is* exophoric, it must function as some variety of situational exophoric, much more often than as formal exophoric. This situation is qualitatively different from English, where S-ellipsis is either endophoric or predominantly formal. The fact that exophoric S-ellipsis may have an intended S-segment which refers not to the interactants but the third person—appropriately referred to in Urdu as Gaeb (absent)—adds greatly to the opacity of this implicit device.

5.6.4 Restricted exophoric ellipsis in Urdu

Operating again with the optimal and non-optimal degrees of implicitness (see 5.5.2–5.5.3), let us examine exophoric S-ellipsis in Urdu. If such ellipsis functions as instantial exophoric—i.e. at a non-optimal degree of implicitness—then the casual listener is likely to interpret the message quite correctly as long as he has access to the material situational setting. When however such ellipsis occurs as restricted exophoric, access to the material situational setting is of no consequence, since the clues needed for the interpretation are in the knowledge shared by the interactants.

If we can find examples of restricted exophoric S-ellipsis where the semantic structure of the message(s) indicates quite clearly that the intended S-segment must refer to some absent third person entity, then we have a case of the highest degree of implicitness—such as is not found in English, since here only the of the third person pronoun might function as restricted exophoric. However, as I have argued above (5.4.2) ellipsis is inherently more implicit than either of the latter mentioned devices. It remains then to find examples of extended discourse which would be acceptable to Urdu speakers and which contain the above feature; below I present two such examples:

36.- sǝlam-o-lǝy-kwm sahyb!
    salam-o-laikum Saheb
    Greetings   Sir!   (i.e. Good morning/afternoon/evening)

  - valǝykwmǝssǝlam bhai! ys dǝfǝ bhi ghǝr pǝr nǝhi hɔ̄y?
    walaikum-as-salam brother! this time too home at not are
    Greetings! is/aren't (—) at home this time, either?

  - nǝhī ji. ǝbhi ǝbhi bahǝr gǝe hɔ̄y.
    not sir now now out went are
    no, sir! (—) just went out a minute ago.

  - to   kya xǝbǝr hǝy? dehli ja rǝhe hɔ̄y ky nǝhī?
    then what news is? Delhi go ing is that not
    what's the news then? Is/are (—) going to Delhi, or not?

  - ji ǝpǝn ko to kwch pǝtǝ nǝhī;   kǝl   teliphun kiya tha.
    sir me to   some know not; yesterday telephone did was
    I don't know sir! (—) did telephone yesterday.

  - ǝccha aē   to bǝta dena ky hǝm ae the.
    o.k. come then tell give that I came was
    o.k. when (—) come(s), then tell (—) that I called.

37.- kyɔ̄ bhǝi ǝb kys lie ae ho?
    why   now which for come are
    Now then, why are (you) here again?

  - sǝrkar vǝhi   pǝreshani hǝy; tin mǝhine se   tǝnxah
    master the same worry   is; three months since wages
    Sir, its the same worry; for the last three months (my) wages

    rwki hǝy; mɔ̄y soca ap bol dē to shayd jǝldi   kǝr
    stopped are; I thought you speak give then perhaps quickly do
    have been with-held; I thought if you tell (*—) then perhaps

    dē; bǝcce bhuke hɔ̄y.
    give kids hungry are
    (—) might hurry. (my) kids are going hungry.

  - pucha twm ne kyɔ̄ roki hǝy?
    asked you   why stopped is
    did you ask why (—) have stopped (*your wages)?

  - ji sǝrkar bole ki tin hǝfte ki jo chwTTi bimari
    yes sir said that three weeks of that leave sickness
    yes Sir, (—) said that because of the three weeks' sickness

    ki li thi to ws me kǝT gǝi.
    of took was then that in cut went
    leave that (—) took, (—) will have to make up for it.

In the above examples ellipsis is indicated by round brackets in the English translations. Not all of these represent S-ellipsis; and not all brackets are unfilled. There are two examples of Complement ellipsis, indicated by placing a star * in the bracket. One of these is filled (37; turn 3; **your wages**); the evidence for this comes from the co-text directly, as the only thing stopped is the wages of the first speaker. Note that the entry is not underlined; underlining is used only to indicate exophoric ellipsis. The other filled bracket is in the same example at Turn 1 (**you**); this is a case of formal exophoric; the form of the P-segment permits one invariable selection **twm**. In the last line of the last turn of this example, we have a border line case. The semantics of the rest of the message in text (37) makes it quite obvious that the penultimate bracket could only have I as the intended S-segment; the form of the P-segment remains opaque since in this clause the concord is with Complement **chwTTi** and not with the intended S-segment. The nature of the dialogue in both examples (36), (37) is such that the referents of the other exophoric S-ellipsis could not possibly be present on the interactive scene. The dialogues are however quite extended, showing that communication is taking place without any problem. Further, the social distance between the interactants is quite different in the two examples: in (36), the first speaker is a friend/relation of the family whose servant of considerable standing is his addressee; the social distance is near minimal. In (37), this distance is much greater: the first speaker is likely to be an employee of a fairly low standing, the second must be a superior with considerable power. This points to the fact that the occurrence of exophoric ellipsis does not correlate with a particular tenor selection. I shall return to the question of the environments in which restricted exophoric ellipsis is less frequent, but before this let us look at an additional source of greater implicitness in Urdu.

5.6.5 Complement ellipsis in Urdu

I have argued that the implicitness of ellipsis is so great because the area in which the intended meanings may lie can only be stated by reference to the elliptical string itself (5.4.2 above). It follows that the less implicit the rest of the syntagm, the easier it would be to retrieve the intended meanings. If, then, a clause with S-ellipsis were to contain also Complement ellipsis, I think we would be justified in claiming greater implicitness for that string. The question of Complement ellipsis was not raised in the discussion of English, because the constraints on such ellipsis are even stronger.

For example, its exophoric functioning is not permitted at all. We cannot say **read?** in English to mean **have you read it?** However, Urdu very often makes use of C-ellipsis along with an S-ellipsis, so that the translation equivalent of **read?** i.e. **pəRh lia?** is a fairly normal and common pattern in Urdu.

There are, of course, some conventionalized, non-productive specimens of exophoric C-ellipsis in English e.g. **finished?**. However, one cannot, by analogy, ask **knitted?** or **made?** or **typed?**. In Urdu, C-ellipsis is a productive pattern; sentences such as **bwn lia?** (knitted), **bən gəya** (made?) or **mil gəya?** (found) and dozens like these occur all the time. I am certainly not implying that Urdu speakers talk in one word sentences as children are supposed to in the holophrastic stage. None the less it is amazing to what extent one finds oneself talking thus to members of one's family, friends, colleagues, and of course one's servants. Here is an example of such an exchange:

38. – pəka lia?
     cooked?   (i.e. have you finished cooking it?)

   – hã
     yes.   (yes)

   – cəkhao zəra
     give a taste   (let me have a little taste)

   – lijie
     have   (here you are)

   – bəhwt məze ka həy; tez   āc pər əb nə rəkkho;
     very   taste of is   high flame on now no keep
     is very tasty; don't put on high flame now.

     xərab ho   jae ga; bəlke mere xyal   se ys pyale
     bad become go will rather my thought with this bowl
     will get spoilt; I'd say take out in this bowl.

     mẽ nykal   lo.
     in   turn out take
     (it's very tasty; don't put it on high flame any more; it will get
     spoilt; I'd say perhaps you should take it out in this bowl)

I doubt if any normal speaker of Urdu will find this exchange either extraordinary or incomprehensible, even though without the situational clues the precise meaning of C-ellipsis is not available.

5.6.6 The semantic style of Urdu

As planned earlier (5.6.1) I have started by an examination of the logically highest degree of implicitness in Urdu—that which arises from a substantial use of exophoric ellipsis, in particular of restricted exophoric ellipsis. I hope that the previous discussions have established beyond doubt the fact that the system of the language permits a much higher degree of implicitness than that permitted by the system of English. Of course Urdu has other implicit devices than those of ellipsis; but since we can make this point of greater implicitness simply through an examination of the patterns of ellipsis, there is no need to describe these other implicit devices, though it is my impression that comparable differences will be found in other areas too.

Let us now turn to the second question: what is the range of environments in which the optimal degree of implicitness might be employed by the Urdu speaker? The claim that the system permits a very high degree of implicitness is not tantamount to the claim that therefore every speaker of that language **must** exploit this potential. In English the clause pattern exemplified by **would that they offered me a million pounds** is permitted, but it could not be described as offering a resource which is typically and regularly exploited by any members of the contemporary English speaking community. Similarly, being permitted to use a high degree of implicitness is not equal to being forced to use it. Otherwise the case for arguing cultural control on semantic styles would be weaker; nor could we explain how the same system of language can serve the differing needs of different sub-cultures, sharing the same language. Because of this, there is a significance to the claim that not only does the system of Urdu language permit a much higher degree of implicitness than English does, but also the speakers of the language employ this same degree of implicitness in a wide range of contexts.

We can claim without hesitation that the dominant semantic style in Urdu is the implicit one, because the range of environments in which this style can be used appropriately without raising communicative problems is much wider than that where it could not be used so. This latter range can be specified very simply as those contexts where the access to the language is through the written channel and the field is (semi)technical, for example textbooks on history, chemistry, etc. will not display the use of exophoric ellipsis. For the remaining range of contexts, it is my impression that neither class membership nor social distance affect the frequency of restricted exophorics.

To say, then, that one is an Urdu speaker is largely to discount the possibility of being misunderstood. It is to believe that your addressee knows what you are on about; it is to assume that the chances of ambiguity are so low as to be almost negligible. This raises a fascinating problem: how do we decide what can be ambiguous? How can we decide what is or is not universally grammatical? If in English it is grammatical to say **must be cooked** in the presence of a pan of rice on the stove, it surely cannot be ungrammatical to say the same sentence in the absence of the pan. Grammars may or may not be pot-boilers, but the question of grammaticality cannot be made to depend upon the presence or absence of a pan of rice on the stove! The environment can only be taken into account in a systematic manner if the boundary between language and non-language is not water-tight, if grammar is seen as a mode of meaning, and meaning itself as fundamentally the use of language in the living of life. Without such systematic relations, one can only invoke *ad hoc* rules. Thus pragmatics will tell us that the speaker's communicative competence consists in avoiding ambiguity and that ambiguity in this case is avoided if the pan is physically present on the interactive scene; clearly this is 'natural logic'.

These assumptions and modes of descriptions would be quite harmless but for the fact that normally along with them goes the assumption that the natural logic of situations is the same the world over. If you are a rational being you know what is 'obvious', what is not; what is given, what is new. The comparison of English and Urdu does not support these assumptions. The invariant natural logic of the situation does not prevent an Urdu speaker from saying:

39. zərə dekho to bavərci-xane mē̃! pək gəya ho ga.
     little look   kitchen   in cooked gone become will
     just take a look into the kitchen! must be cooked.
     (i.e. go to the kitchen and take a look at the thing you know
     I am talking about because I rather think it must be cooked.)

Subscribing to the tenet of a universal natural logic, we must either see the Urdu speaker as maddeningly illogical—primitive, perhaps?—or we must cook up a romantic hypothesis about all members of the culture possessing a sixth sense that allows them to ESP the more precise intended meanings: such sentimental adulation of the politico-economically underprivileged groups is not entirely absent from the sociolinguistic literature. But clearly there is little to choose between these two science fiction views. Nor do I wish to give the impression that if understanding meanings in English is a miracle—as some theories of semantics would have us believe—then it is a wellnigh impossible feat to perform in Urdu. Unlike many American Indian cultures (Benedict 1935), the culture here is not a silent one; nor is there any reason to believe that communication suffers more breakdowns in Urdu than it does in English. What all this means is that somehow the addressee must be able to retrieve the information which the speaker refers to only implicitly because he expects the addressee to know. This successful transaction of meaning is 'neither a miracle nor a mirage' (Geertz 1971); it is something made possible through participation in the same culture.

Sources of ambiguity cannot be defined in isolation from specific cultures. What we perceive as a universally applicable natural logic because it applies invariably in our own linguistic universe might be simply a culturally specific way of saying, being and behaving. Meanings and ways of meaning are a function of man's ability to construct symbolic systems—perhaps the only species-specific innate attribute. But there is no conclusive evidence that the meanings meant by humanity are entirely derived from and predictable as a result of the brute aspects of the physical world in which man lives. To understand language at its deepest level, we must see it primarily as a cultural phenomenon wherein systems of meaning appear not because the 'real' world is thus and thus, but because the world has been construed thus and thus by specific sub-groups of humanity; and this construed world *is* their real world. But what does it mean to say that sources of ambiguity must be defined by reference to a culture?

5.7 LANGUAGE AND SOCIAL SYSTEMS

5.7.1 Social factors in the interpretation of implicit styles

If it is true that interactions of the type exemplified by (36) and (37) are fairly normal, what allows an ordinary Urdu speaker to operate on the same wave length as the speaker? We cannot invoke a high degree of intimacy between the specific interactants (cp. 37), so the answer appears unavoidable that in some sense the Urdu speaker's world must be a fairly well-regulated place in which persons, objects and processes have well-defined positions with reference to each other, and the speakers know the details. Let me make this point by reference to a familiar situation.

If **has he already left?** when addressed to my boss's secretary would normally be interpreted by her as **has my boss left?**, this is largely because there is a routine, a well-defined set of relationships whereby the secretary is expected to know about my boss, who is expected to be in that particular place at certain times of the days of the week and the secretary expects to be asked about the boss but not about scores of other males that might be milling around in that same building. These expectations are not 'natural' in the way that mountains are natural; they were constructed by groups of men and women. Their construction created a set of roles; culture consists of a socially created, mutually recognized set of rights and obligations centring around systems of roles.

However, role systems can vary in respect of how well defined their boundaries are: i.e. how clearly established the rights and obligations accruing to the role are. Obviously the more determinate these boundaries, the less likely it is that ambiguity will arise in social interaction. I am suggesting that the role system for the community of Urdu speakers is considerably more determinate than it is for the middle-class English speaker. It is only this kind of social structure which will explain why the optimally implicit style has such wide currency in the community. We must postulate that the set of expectations regarding who does what, when, where, why and in relation to whom must be fairly well established.

I am well aware that emphasis on highly determinate role systems is liable to be misunderstood—there is a danger that one is treating 'individuals' as if they were marionettes. Let me add, then, that individuation is not the strong feature of the Indo-Pakistani cultures; or rather, the conception of individuality is fundamentally different. Secondly, a role system can be highly determinate at one level without being so at another. Thus there is a much greater consensus in the 'picture' of the rights and obligations of the various roles than there is adherence to this picture in the actual practices of every member of the community. So, even in the presence of divergent cultural practices in the modern era, the picture associated with each role remains largely intact. A role in the Indo-Pakistani cultures is a sharply defined object with hardly any fuzziness to its boundaries so far as its popular picture is concerned; how that role is enacted today and what consequences it might have on the total culture is a different matter. It is by postulating a large consensus in the picture of the role that we can explain the lack of ambiguity in the following examples:

40. əy-həy! dekho to Gwsəlxane ki kya   halət həy!
     gosh   look do   toilet   of what condition is
     Gosh Look what condition the toilet is in!

     barə bəj gəy   əbhi tək nəhi ai.   zərə dekho
     twelve ring went up-to-now   not came little look
     it's twelve o'clock and (she) is still not arrived. Just

     kəhã   Gaeb ho gəi
     where disappear become went
     find out where (she) has disappeared to.

41. ɔre bhɔi kɔhã   cɔli   gaĩ? mere kɔpRe tɔk nɔhĩ nykale.
    hello   where walked went? my clothes   not taken-out.
    hello, where have (—) got to? (—) not even taken out my clothes.

    nɔhane ko bɔyTha hũ. der   ho   jae gi.
    bathe   to sitting am. late become go will.
    (I) am sitting waiting to have my bath. (—) will get late.

Any reader who truly knows the sub-continent will understand these two examples qualitatively differently from those who do not have a picture of the roles involved. In (40), the she will be understood as referring to bhɔngɔn (a woman whose job is to clean the toilet); further they will understand the sentences to have been addressed to a servant; the speaker, on the other hand, must be a woman of the house. In (41), the speaker has to be a husband and the addressee his wife. This degree of specificity comes as a result of having a picture of the role of a wife; note that the P-segments cɔli gɔĩ and nykale provide no unambiguous clue about the intended S-segment.

5.7.2 Role systems and their non-verbal manifestations

Interesting though the question is, I shall not ask here what gives rise to such determinate role systems. The answer could be offered in terms of religion creating an overall 'ethos' (Geertz 1973), or types of social solidarity (Durkheim 1947; Bernstein 1971) arising from the distribution of labour, or affective structures which are the product of dominant kinship dyads (Hsu 1963, 1971) or by some other hypothesis (Benedict 1935; Douglas 1972). The parameters that are important to the definition of determinate roles consist of ascribed attributes (Bernstein 1971). Thus the inherent attributes of sex, age, age-relation, and other inherited factors e.g. caste, religion, and family's social status function as the determiners of the roles. The centrality of all these factors to the roles on the sub-continent is indisputable. What are the non-verbal ways of 'legitimizing' these attributes, so that they do not lose their hold in the definition of the role system?

Consider the construction of social hierarchy. Despite determined efforts in recent years, caste remains an important vector in determining hierarchy. In 1981, an entire colony of scheduled caste were burnt out of home and house because some of them had dared to pass lewd remarks about an unmarried girl of the upper caste. This is all the more significant if we remember that males passing lewd remarks about females is not an entirely extraordinary happening on the sub-continent; quite the contrary. Within the family, hierarchy is strictly determined by age-relation and sex. Thus both caste and kinship operate as definers of roles (Mayer 1960; Dumont 1966; Mandelbaum 1970).

Turning to the socialization of the young, we shall find that much emphasis is laid on categories of behaviour which are defined by reference to sex, age, kinship relation, and family status (Hsu 1963; Strodtbeck 1971; Hasan 1975). The patterns of how leisure might be used are different for the two sexes; the behaviour of the sister to the brother is not one of 'equality', and so on.

The institution of marriage again upholds the sanctity of these boundaries. The choice of a marriage partner is a process of delicate balancing of caste, class—economic and social—and prestige status of the two families. To marry into a family below one's own in any of these respects is to be subjected to shame; and the shame is greater if the woman moves below the status of her father's family.

I hope it is apparent from these brief remarks that the entire weight of behaviour in the community is orientated towards sensitizing members to the rights and obligations of others—where in the last analysis these rights and obligations accrue from their hierarchic location in the social structure. Despite the slow and constant introduction of a conflicting view of social relations, I believe I am right in suggesting that the Urdu speakers' world remains to a large extent a world in which everyone's place is well known in respect of any one they could possibly come in social contact with.

It is just possible that this description arouses either a sense of claustrophobia in my reader or a feeling of womb-like security. However, I am concerned neither with denigrating the suffocating impersonality of existence nor the warm security of knowing who you are. The moon has a dark side to it, as I believe Douglas remarked (1972), whether it is the lonely individuation of the middle-class English speaker or the public communality of the Urdu speaker. My concern is simply to establish that the two cultures are qualitatively different; and that this difference is reflected in their characteristic semantic styles. Further, the peculiarities of the social structure are essential for explaining the peculiarities of the semantic style.

5.7.3 Social structure and language system.

Summing up my position on the semantic style of Urdu, I would say that the optimal degree of implicitness in style is a function of the social structure of the speech community; moreover, the consideration that appears to be the regulating principle is that of creating clear role boundaries. This highly implicit style is capable of surviving because the role system maintains highly determinate boundaries, regarding which there is a great deal of communal consensus. It is certainly not a part of the communal expectation that 'you are free to do your own thing'. As the language puts it proverbially, even god cannot be worshipped in a mosque built of your own private brick and a half. The verbal style is in keeping with patterns of non-verbal behaviour, which again support the same maintenance of clear boundaries. The case for this dialectic between the social structure and the semantic style is strengthened if it can be shown that the system of Urdu language possesses other attributes directly relatable to the characterizing attributes of the social structure.

In this respect the first characteristic of Urdu that comes to mind is that which has often been described as 'levels' of speech in socio-linguistic literature. Often the contrast is presented of the pronominal system in the language, where the pronouns are said to be formal or informal (Khubchandani 1975), but the matter goes far beyond the pronominals, if we are concerned with the relation between wording and meaning. The obsession with hierarchy that Geertz (1960) finds among the Javanese does not seem to be specific to the Javanese alone. The Urdu speaking community too strikes a delicate balance between age, sex, status of the family, and degree of acquaintance to decide what level of speech is to be used, how a person is to be addressed or referred to. It is this concern which finds its expression in the appropriate use of the honorific forms of speech—which again transcend the boundary of the pronominal system, even at the level of wordings.

The use of the honorific form is determined by reference to kinship relation, age-relation, socio-economic status, and prestige status —the latter is not always determined by the socio-economic status. In the pronoun system, the option honorific vs. non-honorific is not applicable to the first person pronoun: the speaker acts as a point by reference to which the lower and the higher is measured along the various attribute scales mentioned above. Even where a non-honorific term e.g. **xadym** (servant) is used to refer to self, this selection is conditioned by the status of the addressee *vis-à-vis* oneself. The attributes, themselves, are capable of being ordered with regard to their relevance. Kinship and age take precedence over all considerations: no matter how poor, how ill-to-do one's uncle may be, he deserves the honorofic form. The middle-class Urdu-speaker will not say **mera cɔca aya** but **mere cɔca ae**. This is, in effect, a way of showing one's estimate of the family status. If the families are equal in prestige and economic status, then age takes on significance; someone older than oneself from a family of equal or higher status, deserves an honorific form.

When the interaction of the system of formality with that of honorifics is examined, we find that formality of speech level always goes with the honorific form. To put it more accurately, the distinction is neutralized. This makes sense in view of the semantics of formality. The choice of formal/informal is applicable only to the interactant roles, since formality is clearly the product of interactant relationship. The actual choice is determined by the degree of social distance: the wider the distance between the two, the more formal the level. In effect, social distance itself is a function of the degree of familiarity, but this familiarity is a meaningful notion only in the environment of family parity. The less intimate one is with an interactant who is one's equal the more likely it is that he is deserving of the honorific form—also that he should be addressed with the formal speech level. Thus the various social vectors for the classification of roles in the society find their expression in the verbal system; and they do this not only through the specific forms associated with the verb or the pronouns but also in the selection of the level of lexicon.

The congruence between the verbal and non-verbal behaviour of the Urdu speakers appears to be such as to justify the statement that the semiotic style of the community is characteristically implicit, that both verbal and non-verbal modes of behaviour are governed by a consideration of the maintenance of clear boundaries. This obsession with the maintenance of clear boundaries appears to act as one of the regulating principles in the social life of the community, and it finds its expression in the ways of being, doing and saying—in other words it exercises a control on the style of meaning.

Compared with this, the regulating principle in the social universe of the middle-class English speaker is indeed very different. Instead of clearly defined ascribed role systems, his social universe contains a challenge—the roles must be achieved (Bernstein 1971) and individuation functions as one of the regulating principles. Whereas the ascribed roles create a secure identity (Hsu 1971; Bernstein 1971), the achieved roles demand the creation of one's identity. The freedom to define one's identity and one's role relation with others carries with it the penalty that nothing much can be taken for granted; ambiguity can therefore exist and must be guarded against. The world is not necessarily a well-regulated, stable place; one's own self has to act as the catalyst. This is not a social environment in which a high degree of implicitness could be tolerated—and it is not.

5.7.4 Implicit style in English speaking community

If the above explanations of the social genesis and function of the implicit style of meaning is accepted, it would follow that the English speaking sub-community whose characteristic semantic style is implicit—i.e. Bernstein's restricted code users—must experience a social relationship qualitatively nearer that of the Urdu speaker than that of its middle-class counterpart. It is at this point that the question cannot be avoided: why and how do these social relations arise? What changes them? The Durkheimian explanation in terms of forms of social solidarity is one such effort. It seems to me that approaching the problem as I have done raises many interesting questions. What attributes does a social structure have to have to contain within itself two such sub-communities? What kind of relations can exist between these two sub-communities? The comparison with the Urdu semantic style is interesting from another point of view: to speak highly implicitly is no more looked down upon in the Urdu speaking universe than r-less-ness would be frowned upon by the Queen. Not so for the sub-community orientated to implicit style in the English speaking community. Why not? Is it because there is some attribute inherently undesirable in this way of saying and meaning, or is it that by contrast with the privileged it presents a dead end? To this, we may provide an answer if we examine the environments both in Urdu and in English communities where the orientation to the implicit style would be inappropriate. I would suggest this examination will allow a basis for stating the direction of cultural change.

5.7.5 Conclusions

I have deliberately chosen the distinction between the implicit and the explicit ways of saying and meaning for the simple reason that so far as the referential content—the experiential meaning—of the message is concerned, it could plausibly be claimed that **John can't swim** and its elliptical version **John can't** mean exactly the same thing. The difference between the two is often treated as a matter belonging to performance, therefore lying in pragmatics—not in semantics—or it is seen as simply concerned with surface structure matters, hence not worthy of serious consideration. I would suggest that both these views are wrong. These dichotomies do not serve any useful purpose. On the other hand, if one treats the ways of saying as being necessarily the ways of meaning, as I have attempted to do, it seems quite plausible to suggest that the relationship between language and social life is deep indeed. Different ways of saying reveal different orientations to orders of relevance—their examination shows how the semantic universe of two communities may not be identical.

Today it is normal to claim equality by claiming identity. But identity is not a necessary condition of equality. The readiness to assert that what 'we' can mean, the 'others' can mean too is often associated with liberal egalitarianism. I would suggest that it could in fact be the result of a harmful lack of sensitivity to differences which are possibly as important for the true appreciation of the 'other' as the laudable fact of their being just like us. After all this latter fact follows from our humanity; but the differences are our own creations through which we manage to maintain our monopolies and our interests.

NOTES

1. This paper is a revised version of a talk presented at the Bourg Wartenstein Symposium No. 66, 8–17 August 1975.
2. The conventions used here are borrowed from Firth in Harley (1944), with the following alterations: vowel nasalization indicated by diacritic above vowel thus aũ; sh for ʃ ; G for ɣ ; capital letters for retroflexion e.g. T for t and R for ɽ , etc.

BIBLIOGRAPHY

Benedict, R. (1935), *Patterns of Culture*, London, Routledge & Kegan Paul.
Bernstein, B. B. (1971), *Class, Codes and Control*, Vol. 1, London, Routledge & Kegan Paul.
Berry, M. (1975–7), *Introduction to Systemic Linguistics*, Vols. 1 and 2, London Batsford.
Bolinger, D. (1968), *Aspects of Language*, New York, Harcourt Brace & World.
Brown, R. W. (1970), *Psycholinguistics: Selected Papers*, Chicago, Free Press.
Cole, P. and Morgan, J. L. (eds) (1975), *Syntax and Semantics: Vol. 3 Speech Acts*, New York, Academic Press.
Douglas, M. (1972), 'Self-evidence', Henry Myers Lecture given for the Royal Anthropological Institute, 4 May: reprinted in *Implicit Meanings*, London, Routledge & Kegan Paul, 1975, 276–318.
Durkheim, E. (1947), *The Division of Labour in Society*, trs. Simpson, Chicago, Free Press.
Dumont, L. (1966), *Homo Hierarchicus: The Caste System and Its Implications*, trs. Sainsbury, London, Weidenfeld and Nicolson.

Fateh Mohd. Khan (1945), *Misbah-ul-Qawaid, Hissa Doem*, Rampur, Nazim Barqi Press.

Firth, J. R. (1944), 'Introduction' to A. H. Harley, *Colloquial Hindustani*, London, Kegan Paul, Trench, Truber & Co., ix-xxx.

Firth, J. R. (1950), 'Personality and language in society', *Sociological Review* (Journal of the Institute of Sociology), 42, section 2. Also in *Papers in Linguistics*, London, Oxford University Press, 1957.

Geertz, C. (1960), *The Religion of Java*, Chicago, Free Press.

Geertz, C. (ed.) (1971), *Myth, Symbol and Culture*, New York, Norton.

Geertz, C. (1973), *The Interpretation of Culture*, New York, Basic Books.

Grice, H. P. (1975), 'Logic and conversation' in Cole and Morgan, (eds) (1975).

Halliday, M. A. K. (1967-8), 'Notes on theme and transitivity in English', *Journal of Linguistics*, 3:1, 37-81; 3:2, 199-244; 4:2, 179-216.

Halliday, M. A. K. (1970), 'Language structure and language function' in Lyons, (ed.) (1970), 140-65.

Halliday, M. A. K. (1974), *Language and Social Man*, London, Longmans.

Halliday, M. A. K. (1975), *Learning How to Mean*, London, Edward Arnold.

Halliday, M. A. K. (1982), 'A short introduction to functional grammar', Sydney University, mimeo.

Halliday, M. A. K. and Hasan, R. (1976), *Cohesion in English*, London, Longmans.

Halliday, M. A. K. and Hasan, R. (1980), *Text and Context: Aspects of Language in a Semiotic Social-Perspective*, Sophia Linguistica VI, Sophia University, Tokyo.

Hasan, R. (1972), 'The verb BE in Urdu' in J. M. W. Verhaar, (ed.), *The Verb BE and Its Synonyms*, Part 5, Dordrecht, D. Reidel.

Hasan, R. (1973), 'Code register and social dialect' in *Codes, Class and Control*, Vol. 2, London, Routledge & Kegan Paul.

Hasan. R. (1976), 'Socialization and cross-cultural education', *International Journal of Social Linguistics*, 8.

Hasan, R. (1978), 'Text in the systemic functional model' in W. U. Dressler, (ed.), *Current Trends in Textlinguistics*, Berlin, De Gruyter.

Hasan, R. (1980), 'What's going on: a dynamic view of context in language' in *The Seventh LACUS Forum*, Columbia, Hornbeam Press.

Hasan, R. (1981), 'Coherence and cohesive harmony' in J. Flood, ed., *Understanding Reading Comprehension*, forthcoming.

Hsu, F. L. K. (1963), *Class, Caste and Club*, Princeton, N.J., Van Nostrand.

Hsu, F. L. K. (ed.) (1971), *Kinship and Culture*, Chicago, Aldine.

Hsu, F. L. K. (1971), 'Psychosocial homeostasis and Jen: Conceptual tools for advancing psychological anthropology', *American Anthropologist*, 73:1.

Ishfaq Ahmed (n.d.) *ek mohabbət səw əfsane*, Lahore, Latif Publishers.

Kachru, Y. (1966), 'An introduction to Hindi syntax', University of Illinois, mimeo.

Khubchandani, L. (1975), 'Toward a selection grammar: fluidity in modes of address and reference in Hindi', Honolulu, East-West Centre, mimeo.

Labov, W. (1970), 'The logic of non-standard English', in F. Williams, (ed.), *Language and Poverty*, Chicago, Markham.

Leech, G., (1974), *Semantics*, Harmondsworth, Penguin.

Lenneberg, E. (1971) 'Language and cognition' in Steinberg and Jakobovits (eds) (1971), 536-57.

Lyons, J. (1970), *New Horizons in Linguistics*, Harmondsworth, Penguin.

Mandlebaum, D. G. (1970), *Society in India*, Vols 1-2, Berkeley, University of California Press.

Mayer, A. C. (1960), *Caste and Kinship in Central India: A Village and Its Religion*, London, Routledge & Kegan Paul.

Steinberg, D. D. and Jakobovits, L. A., (eds) (1971), *Semantics: An Interdisciplinary Reader in Philosophy, Linguistics and Psychology*, Cambridge, Cambridge University Press.

Strodtbeck, F. L. (1971), 'Sex-role identity and dominant kinship relations' in Hsu, (ed.) (1971).

Verma, S. K. (1961), 'A study in the systemic description of Hindi grammar and comparison of the Hindi English verbal group', University of Edinburgh doctoral thesis, unpublished.

Wittgenstein, L. (1921), *Tractatus Logico-Philosophicus*, London, Routledge & Kegan Paul.

Whorf, B. L. (1956), *Language, Thought and Reality, Selected Writings*, edited by J. B. Carroll, Cambridge, Mass., MIT Press.

Young, D. J. (1980), *The Structure of English Clauses*, London, Hutchinson.

Index